VERONESE

THIS VOLUME EDITED BY ANDRÉ
GLOECKNER WAS FIRST PUBLISHED
IN FEBRUARY MCMXL BY THE
HYPERION PRESS, PARIS. COLOUR
BLOCKS ENGRAVED BY CLICHÉS-
UNION AND REH, PARIS ; TEXT
AND COLOUR PLATES PRINTED BY
G. DESGRANDCHAMPS, PARIS. PHO-
TOGRAVURE BY HUMBLOT, NANCY.
BINDING BY JOSEPH TAUPIN, PARIS.

VERONESE

BY

ANTOINE ORLIAC

TRANSLATED FROM THE FRENCH

BY

MARY CHAMOT

THE HYPERION PRESS

LONDON   PARIS   NEW YORK

PRINTED IN FRANCE

COPYRIGHT 1940 BY HYPERION, PARIS

MARRIAGE. British Museum. Photo Braun & Cie.

VERONESE

THE art of Paolo Caliari, a native of Verona, one of the largest and most beautiful cities of Northern Italy, is linked to the purest Venetian tradition. He was not a spontaneous product of his time and environment, but was the result of a rapid decorative evolution, achieved through truth, realism, movement and colour — an evolution which began after Jacopo Bellini broke loose from the framework of Byzantine rigidity.

He is the expression of hieratic constraint relaxing into luminous activity.

The artist spreads before us a pageant of Venetian life which reached its most brilliant point in the Golden Age of the XVIth century, when Venice shone resplendently before the eyes of an astonished world.

For a long time Veronese was looked upon merely as a prodigious decorator, who resolved himself in eminently plastic creations but lacked sensibility; a charmer possessed with a gift to win us by the magic of his colour.

In fact, Veronese never relied on the strain of sentiment to which so many artists owe their relative and facile success. One seldom fails to win over the majority when stirring the depths of the human heart. It is another matter to touch and thrill the intelligence, to arouse higher emotions revealing unsuspected horizons.

The art of Veronese is as seductive and haughty as his character, and much more intellectual than is generally admitted. The charm with which he holds the spectator is only a pretext to lead him further into profound analysis.

He succeeded in putting the resourcefulness of a perfect technique at the disposal of his strong, directing mind. This is the privilege of the few aristocrats of art. Leonardo did the same, when he wanted to reveal a domain of mystery and abstraction.

Mantegna's symbolism did more than touch Veronese. The Venetian learnt from the master of Padua the great lesson by which Giovanni Bellini had already profited. But while Mantegna, steeped in classicism, delighted in allegory and knew how to animate conventional figures with poetry, Veronese created a spiritual spectacle behind the moving curtain of the ardent and factitious pleasure of Venetian life and thereby proved himself to be the most modern painter of his time.

The Inquisition was far-seeing when it accused him of mingling religious subjects with representations of his own day, and though these were perhaps not heretical, they were certainly significant.

First Veronese freed himself from the tradition of narrow mysticism, which the Latin Church inherited from her enemy the Greek Church. After having painted men of the past he painted those of his century, leaving to secret symbolism the care of separating the significant characters from the rest. His answer to the Inquisition was full of subtlety: " We painters take the same liberties as poets and madmen. "

Was Veronese really charmed and carried away by his environment ? Did he love it as much as has been assumed ? Did he paint only with the sensuousness and rapture of a colourist steeped in the joys of light ?

To give such a brilliant synthesis of life it was necessary for him to dominate his epoch with all the force of his innermost solitude and intelligence.

II. THE TEACHERS OF VERONESE

A truly gifted painter seeking to express himself cannot assimilate the gifts and mannerisms of one master only. His personality is evolved in the midst of complex influences. Who were the teachers of Veronese ? Little is known about his youth and early work. Born in Verona in 1528, son of Gabriele di Piero Caliari, a sculptor and stone-cutter, he probably worked in his father's atelier, for he first learned to model figures in clay. His boyhood was spent in his native town of Verona, surrounded by turreted walls with fortified bridges spanning the Adige.

He spent several years in copying engravings by Albert Dürer and Lucas van Leyden and drawings by Parmigianino.

One of his uncles, Antonio Badile (1516-1560) was a good painter; though his fame was eclipsed by the glory of his great disciple, the quality of his work deserved a better fate.

The works of Badile clearly show the value of his teaching. He painted several religious subjects, notably a *Madonna and Saints* (1546), the *Raising of Lazarus* and a *Death of Christ* (1556), now in the Pinacoteca in Verona, and an admirable *Presentation in the Temple* in the Pinacoteca in Turin, which prove that Badile's art fascinated his nephew and helped to decide his vocation.

Young Paolo attended his uncle's studio and that of Giovanni Caroto (1491-1555) another Veronese painter and architect, whose *Madonna and Child* in the Louvre is colourful, decorative and full of charm.

There were two schools of painting at that time in Verona : one headed by Paolo Morando Cavazzola (1489-1522) who was formed in the school of the XVth century and fortified by the ample style of the XVIth century; he combined vivacity with perfect harmony, had an easy touch and worked in the manner of Pisanello; the other included Antonio Badile, Giovanni Caroto, Francesco Torbido, known as " il moro di Verona " (1483-1565) Giambattista del Moro and Domenico Riccio, known as " il Brussasorci " (1515-1557) all of whom, while retaining certain links with the art of their native town, were influenced by the charm of the Venetian school.

A pupil of Caroto, a great colourist and, according to Berenson, a master of great historical importance owing to his modernism Riccio invented a new method of design and composition using a peculiar system of light without stressing form and line in order to keep the element of colour pure.

He was an ingenious and prolific decorator of palaces and churches and knew well how to combine the memories of Titian, of Giulio Romano, of Michelangelo and of Parmigianino.

Veronese followed all these suggestions and had mastered a sure and personal technique, before coming under the influence of the art of Palma and Titian.

**

Though he was formed independently of Venetian art, young Paolo ended by conferring upon it a new splendour. A long line of artists had prepared his triumph of colour. The whole secret of this attraction is condensed in the rapid and fascinating evolution of Venetian painting.

Whereas in Florence, in Siena and in Umbria the art of the Middle Ages passed from the Byzantine tradition to mystical and symbolical humanism, then on to realistic vision, tempered with fifteenth century classicism, becoming more conventional and decorative with the Renaissance, Venetian painting up to the sixteenth century continued to follow the technique of the Greek mosaicists, working within the narrow limits of the Byzantine canon. In the fourteenth century Venice had not yet felt the timid surging of the new blood, such as circulated in Giotto's frescoes. At the beginning of the fifteenth century, the Venetians still ignored the lesson of the Assisan painter. They lingered over Madonnas clad in stiff robes, and over emaciated saints on a golden background. And suddenly, passing over the intermediary stage of fresco, they turned from mosaics to painting on canvas.

The Venetian genius expressed itself eventually with the help of the arid realism of Carlo Crivelli, the keen observation and technique of the Flemish school (which was introduced by Antonello da Messina) the symphonies in black, red and gold of Paolo Uccello, prodigious painter of battle-scenes, the peaceful rhythm of colours and lines that Piero della Francesca inherited from Angelico, the picturesque narrative, the lightness, the sumptuous vision of Gentile da Fabriano and the magnificent cavalcades of Benozzo Gozzoli, awed by the gorgeous train of the Emperor of the East.

It found its equilibrium with the robust and greatly gifted art of those dynasties of painters, the Vivarini and Bellini, noble artists of consummate ability, who painted as naturally as one breathes.

Little by little they released Venice from the Umbrian, Tuscan and Lombard influences, by assimilating them and restoring them with a new originality; they gave their city a regal art and prepared the splendid feast of colour to which the whole of the XVIth century was invited.

Gentile da Fabriano, who belonged to the mystical Sienese school, worked in Venice with Pisanello da Verona, himself a pupil of Andrea del Castagno. Both were highly gifted, full of the joy of living, taking heed of lordly magnificence, and they both brought the vision of Rome and Florence to Venice with the taste for pomp, pageantry and brilliant processions.

Pisanello enriched Venetian painting with the tradition of the French and German illuminators. He brought with him that decisive accent which gave so much character to his medals.

Meanwhile in Padua, so close to Venice, Donatello gave the signal of the Renaissance by his energetic modelling, releasing his bronze figures from the stylized Gothic stiffness.

Mantegna recalled this in the precise science of his expressive foreshortening, until he came to Venice and steeped himself in the joy of colour. He married the daughter of old Jacopo Bellini, emphasized the influence of Gentile da Fabriano and hastened the dislocation of Byzantine hieraticism. Through his brother-in-law Giovanni Bellini, he transmitted the ease and Dionysian intoxication of Greek art to Giorgione.

Henceforth a current of freedom flows through all Venetian painting. The sulphurous light that Gentile Bellini inherited from the Moslem vision is miraculously developed in Carpaccio's work : the motley crowds, the richly draped figures, the turbaned heads, the high buildings, the brightly-decked vessels, already caressed by the cooler azure of Bellini, are now warmed with amber vibrations and appear in a play of picturesque colour.

With Giovanni and Gentile Bellini and Carpaccio all the symphony, all the rapture of Oriental colour begins to rise in the Venetian sky, where Giorgione, Titian, Palma, Veronese and Tintoretto were to shine. It is the new glory of Venice lighting up.

The rigidity of Byzantine art gradually became more supple and, animated with the breath of life, melted in the golden heat with which Giorgione warmed the truly Athenian grace of those beautiful bodies, rich in youth and health.

Bellini's Virgins became more humanly majestic, expressed charm, a kind of purity and lonely grandeur, which was enhanced by the luminous landscapes. The nude asserted itself victoriously in a calm attitude full of chastity, such as the sensual but restrained Titian and the stormy and tormented Tintoretto sought in vain to recapture.

Venetian painting blossomed forth like a marvellous flower, after having been closely bound by its corselet, and it was Veronese who liberated its joy of living, expressing it in a colourful song.

*_**

If the art of Giovanni Bellini and his pupils Titian and Palma Vecchio found an echo in Veronese, it is certainly Bonifazio dei Pitati who effected the transition. Born in Verona in 1487, a pupil of Palma and a contemporary of Cariani and Lorenzo Lotto, he went to Venice at the age of eighteen where he married Antonio Palma's niece and collaborated with him in several works.

Under Palma Vecchio he lost some of the Veronese influence. He was a prolific and passionate painter, a brilliant colourist possessing the sense of beautiful composition; he painted Biblical subjects but these were a mere pretext for showing the opulent pageantry of Venetian life.

The *Finding of Moses*, as well as the *Parable of Dives and Lazarus* both in the Brera Gallery, Milan, are a preface to the art of Paolo Veronese.

Facile composition, a sense of architecture, a taste for idle and ostentatious luxury, a limpid atmosphere, spacious backgrounds enriched with columns and trees, elegant cavaliers, musicians, servants, deformed dwarfs, dogs, horses, the majesty of the ensemble, the rich details, is there not something in all this which already announces, though less ably, the style and treatment of Veronese?

Though the two pictures in the Louvre are not so representative, they distinctly establish this connection. They reveal the happy gifts proceeding from Titian and Palma to which Caliari added so much more value and prestige.

The type of Veronese's Christ already emerges. We find here Paolo's palette, the range that he extended by his choice of combinations and the quality of his active vibrations: dark greens, lightened by yellower transparencies, orange tempered by ochre, carmine pink, lemon yellows warmed with lakes, livid greys cooled by silver; all this symphonic ensemble which Veronese lifted out of stagnation to exalt the precious sounds by the brilliance of his incomparable performance.

Let us consider *Christ and the Adultress*. In spite of the dominant red and yellow of the whole, the remarkable attitudes, the gestures, the faces of the Venetian beauties, the admirably executed work of the white draperies, the scenic effect given to the monuments, the recession of the landscape, with the distance blurred, prove how deep must have been the influence of his first masters, besides that of Titian and Palma.

The same qualities stand out in the *Raising of Lazarus* where, in spite of the warm brown, the ivory body of the resurrected man sitting at the side of a composition, built upon expressive diagonals, finds happy echoes in the rosy yellows of the draperies and these accords are supported in the scale of yellows, pinks and reds with ashy blues, broken here and there somewhat brusquely by black silences. Bonifazio dei Pitati was a Veronese by birth, became a Venetian by adoption and taste, but retained the luminous calm of the banks of the Adige in spite of the warm environment of Venice. Though he adopted the Venetian style he retained moderation. He never gave in to the chiaroscuro of Titian or to the rather rich and exaggerated softness of Palma Vecchio. He expressed himself with less grandeur and grace than the master of Serinalta, but shared with him the feeling for the grandiose, and always tried to attain this through his aesthetic inclination as well as in the practice of his art. Nevertheless his orchestration was less sonorous than that of his predecessors.

Bonifazio's work does not compare favourably with other Venetian pictures in the Louvre. But I am pleased to detect in him the eloquent silver greys, the serene luminosity and the airy lightness, which Veronese was to exalt until he rivalled the greatest masters of painting.

I have found in Bonifazio dei Pitati a sense of balance and definite order, a scientific distribution of groups around which air and light flow freely; also a certain conventional immobility in his biblical subjects, despite his modern outlook.

Bonifazio dei Pitati, who died in Venice on the 19th of October 1553, was undeniably a good master of Venetian painting and sometimes his achievement is worthy of the best.

SELF-PORTRAIT.
Library of the École des Beaux-Arts, Paris. Photo Giraudon.

Veronese lent to Pitati's style a nobility, distinction and charm which he had inherited from another source.

At the time Titian reigned supreme in Venice. He imposed his fascinating authority on everyone. He embodied Giovanni Bellini, Giorgione and Palma Vecchio. Half a century of tradition lay behind him, and he enriched it with a large and opulent classicism. He condensed fragmentary and dispersed reality into a sober compact, he composed harmonious expressions of form and combined into a calm poetical synthesis the gifts of his ardent but controlled soul.

There was not a subject which he did not treat in a personal way, whether it be a sacred theme, a celestial vision, a pagan mirage, or beauty, which he brought to life in the warmth of an alcove.

Tintoretto alone escaped the charm and discipline of his master in his stormy and tormented vision. He opposed the violence of his temperament and the fugue of his suggestions to the exact science of the great enchanter.

Veronese in his turn was affected by Titian, but other influences came to him simultaneously. It was through his association with the best masters of Parma that Veronese, always mindful of anything which might be of use to him, developed his aristocratic affinities and created an elegant race with which he peopled his canvases. Correggio and Parmigiano radiated the prestige of their school. What a rich heritage he derived from them : facility of drawing, spirituality of reclining bodies, beautiful faces and draperies crushed by an adroit hand !

Under their very eyes he achieved greater success in the wonderful technique with which they painted pale flesh, fine colour, magical effects of great depth and transparent chiaroscuro.

And Veronese soon freed himself from the majestic breadth of the master of Cadore; he preferred the style of Parma : a lighter and more harmonious fullness.

To gold and purple, to shimmering heat he opposed the quiet silver light of North Italian skies, calmly breathing faces, and an elegant and noble demeanour.

Tintoretto's rather disdainful roughness, his quick and plebeian gestures were ennobled by cold dignity and graceful attitudes. Caliari bathes his figures in a limpid atmosphere; you can feel the freshness of these vast and magnificent compositions. He was not entirely absorbed by Venice; the smiling style of Verona with the limpid colouring of Cavazzola, Caroto and Bonifazio dei Pitati became Venetian but retained the peculiar touching charm and lightness of Correggio and his disciples.

Veronese henceforth became one of the greatest artists to glorify painting. The hard strokes with which Titian modelled his volumes soften and change into fulguration; the thick impasto which gave calm sensuality to the flesh, is lightened and enlivened, and creates skin under which you can see the warm blood circulating : the muscles become softer, and though they remain smooth, are more rounded.

Once freed from the mystery of shadow, the human body is modelled more clearly and offers the beauty of gesture and form, and is tastefully draped in rich materials. Titian's warm voluptuousness and his violent reds and yellow-browns are cooled into shimmering metallic tones by adding ash grey to green. The flesh is less pink and in the shadow takes on a chaster tone. The picture melts into a soft harmony of light and the accents of colour are blended and gradated.

A new aristocracy of tones was born on this palette, sometimes reminiscent of Giovanni Bellini's contrasts and of the imagery of the Umbrian school, but henceforth the flashes of colour were joined in an orchestration in which they either played the dominant role or that of a quiet accompaniment.

Veronese is further removed from the classicism of Bellini and Mantegna and carries us away by the swifter method of Correggio. Titian never left the classic calm except in his battle scenes or bacchanals. Then he passes suddenly without transition from voluptuous 'calm, from the supple gestures of women and the haughty carriage of the men, to the clash of soldiers and horses as to a delirium inspired by a bacchanalian rapture.

While respecting constructive order, Veronese nevertheless establishes a rhythmic movement. One of Lot's daughters, fleeing from the fire of Sodom, stops for a moment to do up her sandal. All Veronese's dynamic force is in this instant of suspense between movement and repose. Even if his figures are immobile they seem to be full of luminous activity.

Paolo soon excelled in aerial composition. He had a taste for the beautiful surrounded by space. By measuring the density of flesh he gives the superhuman bodies poised between two skies a peculiar lightness, as if their pores were saturated with air and upheld by the blues to which he assigns such depth.

He alone possessed to a high degree the art of representing, without any apparent effort or confusion, groups of figures surrounded by luminous atmosphere.

His abundance, his ingenuity, the smiling brightness of his colour, make him a decorator who was often carried away by the play of his skill to such an extent as to be accused of caring little about uplifting the soul.

In the XVIIIth century Tiepolo remembered these brilliant qualities and emphasized them even more by condensing his compositions, and by stressing the vacuity of the skies upon which he inscribed his symbols.

III. THE EARLY WORK OF VERONESE

Little is known about the early paintings of Veronese. Only a few of his works are dated, with the result that we have no certain information except regarding his mature period. And it is extremely difficult to arrive at a chronological sequence amid his prolific output.

Even as a youth he must have attracted the attention of his fellow-citizens and the chapter of San Bernardino commissioned him to paint a *Virgin*. This painting, it was said, earned the young artist a promising notoriety, and soon new commissions poured in. Together with a fellow student Giambattista Farinati, he undertook the decoration of country seats round Vicenza and Verona. The architect Michele Sammichele was impressed by the young men's gifts and procured them these jobs, and we find them in the vicinity of Vicenza, painting the halls of the Portesco Palace so artistically that their reputation was established.

Michele Sammichele loved them as his own sons; it was through him that the decoration of the Soranza Palace at Castelfranco was entrusted to them. Later, the surviving frescoes from this building, including an allegory dated 1551, were transferred to canvas and hung in the Pinacoteca of the Seminary in Venice.

The figures of *Temperance*, *Justice*, *Time* and *Fame* now in the Sacristy of the Duomo, Castelfranco, date from the same period.

The following year, Cardinal Ercole Gonzaga took the young painter to Mantua where the Cathedral had been recently built by Giulio Romano. Together with Paolo Farinati, Brusasorci, called the Titian of Verona, and Battista del Moro, Veronese helped to paint an altar-piece. The *Temptation of St. Anthony* by him is now in the Museum at Caen and is superior in quality to the works of the others.

In 1554 we find him in Venice working with Ponchino and Zelotti on the ceiling of the Sala del Consiglio dei Dieci in the Doges' Palace. His reputation was growing though he was only twenty six years old.

He was commissioned to paint four compositions; five others are attributed to his collaborators. Veronese painted *Juno showering gifts on Venice*, *Youth and Age*, *Venus contemplating Olympus* and *Jupiter fulminating the Vices*. The last picture was taken to France in 1797 and was first hung in the Louvre, then " Musée des Arts, " afterwards " Musée Napoléon " until 1810. Then an attempt was made to place it in its original position on a ceiling in the room of Louis XIV at Versailles; the groups were cut up and separated by bands of sky. During some repairs to the roof of the Château a thunderstorm occurred and the pictures were damaged and had to be removed for restoration. And it was finally decided to re-assemble the parts and hang the painting definitely in the Louvre.

Caliari's love of symbolism already appears in this picture. Must we not see the Consiglio dei Dieci crushing the crimes of extortion, treason and lewdness under this apparent allegory of the Lord of Olympus punishing the rebels ? Michelangelo's influence is manifest here. The plastic qualities reveal the hand of a sculptor's son, himself very fond of plastic relief.

One remains speechless before the virtuosity with which the young man possessed the art of aerial composition, the technique of audacious foreshortening, the play of movement and suppleness in relaxation, the very secret of life.

The manifestation of such a personality inevitably led to independence. Henceforth, Veronese leaves his friends, who had become his rivals, and works on his own.

A countryman of his, the Prior of the Gerolamites Torlioni commissioned him to decorate the church of St. Sebastian. From the moment he started this work, Veronese met with so much approval that the decoration of the whole building was entrusted to him. For twelve years this church became a vast workshop for the painter, and his marvellous genius found its full scope. Later on it was to contain his tomb.

On the ceiling of the Sacristy is a *Coronation of the Virgin*. The large ceiling of the church is decorated with four panels, telling the story of *Esther and Ahasuerus*.

Besides other frescoes which no longer exist, Veronese painted in 1558 the *Annunciation* in the nave, figures of *Sibyls* and *Prophets* and episodes from the *Life and Martyrdom of St. Sebastian*. These pictures place Paolo in the front ranks of the decorators of his time. His triumph was complete on the day he won the competition arranged by the procurators of St. Mark for painting the library ceiling; the golden chain, which is officially given to the winner, was presented to him by Titian in the name of all the other painters. After this memorable event Caliari spent some time in Verona and then returned to Venice.

In 1560 he temporarily interrupted his work in the Venetian churches : his great friends and admirers Daniele Barbaro, patriarch of Aquileia and his brother Marc Anthony invited Paolo to Maser near Treviso where he decorated a large villa Giacomelli built by Palladio and adorned with stucco-work and sculpture by Allessandro Vittoria.

Here Veronese expressed himself freely and gave reign to his full vitality, his creative power, and his gaiety of movement. The galeries are peopled with charming visions of modern muses, clothed in antique fashions, but made of contemporary materials, their bare feet in sandals; they are covered with jewels and flowers and are playing on musical instruments.

In the cupola a radiant earth is surrounded by eight planets. The symbolical themes of the four elements complete the decoration, while the four seasons link up with them harmoniously.

The walls of the other rooms and galeries are covered with allegories, trophies, garlands or happy moralities in which the painter's brush triumphs.

When he had finished this work Paolo accompanied the procurator Girolamo Grimani to Rome whither he was sent by the Republic to the Papal Court. The sight of Michelangelo and Raphael's work and, more especially, the study of the antique masterpieces influenced his style, which became broader and simpler without losing any of its qualities of grace and nobility.

In 1565 Veronese de- signed large cartoons for the mosaics in San Marco. The following year he married the daughter of his first teacher Antonio Badile. And in the next ten years a new list of paintings added to the glory of Caliari.

He painted a *Baptism of Christ* for the High Altar of San Giovanni in Latisana, an admirable *Marriage of Saint*

WATCHFULNESS. Doge's Palace, Collegio, Venice. Photo Alinari.

Catherine for the church of St. Catherine, then an *Adoration of the Shepherds* for the silk-weavers' chapel in the church of the Crocicchieri, now in the church of Santi Giovanni e Paolo.

Verona was enriched by two beautiful paintings, the Marogna *Madonna and Child* and the big *Martyrdom of St. George* for San Giorgio in Braida. For the church of the Umiltà in Venice he painted a ceiling, certain fragments of which, notably an *Annunciation*, a *Nativity* and an *Assumption*, are in the Vienna Museum.

In 1572 he produced a *Feast of St. Gregory* for the refectory of Monte Berico, Vicenza. The *Adoration of the Magi* which belongs to the National Gallery, London, was painted a year later, for the church of St. Sylvester in Venice.

At last in 1575 Veronese, assisted by his brother Benedetto Caliari, painted the *Martyrdom of St. Justina* for the High altar of St. Justina in Padua.

Back in Venice, completely master of his art, Caliari received the glorious consecration which his art deserved. He was so much in demand that he could hardly cope with all the public and private commissions inspite of his great assiduity and prodigious facility. Yet the City of the Doges attracted many painters of repute who had no lack of commissions.

This splendid period in the life of Venice made it possible for her art to achieve profusion and brilliancy, so that it rivalled and even surpassed the art of Rome and Florence.

IV. VERONESE AND THE SPLENDOUR OF VENICE

Since Byzantium failed in her role of spiritual stronghold under the blows of Mahomet II, Venice rose amid the ruins of the Greek Empire of the East and became the outpost of the Christian world, placed as she was at the crossways of two civilizations which contested the sea.

The Greek Church, against whom Venice had struggled, was overthrown by Islam. But the City of the Doges, queen of the Adriatic, still flew the gonfalon of St. Mark, surmounted by the Latin cross in the face of the powerful Ottoman Empire.

For twenty five years during the XVIth century an era of peace followed the fratricidal wars by which Venice maintained her power over her rivals, Padua, Milan, Treviso, and Genoa; their pride and jealousy were such that even in time of need Venice could neither enlist their aid nor share her abundance with them.

For a time she had insured her trade against the

MEEKNESS. Doge's Palace, Collegio, Venice. Photo Alinari.

threats of the Turk. Situated in the centre of important routes, which led across the Alps to Austria, France and the Rhine, she saw all the influence of the Latin, Moslem and German genius converging towards her.

It is true that this peace which she enjoyed was dearly bought. Charles V having momentarily disposed of Francis I by the treaty of Bologna, forced the Venetians to return what they had conquered and pay for their independence, at the same time confirming all their commercial rights on the coast of Naples. He crowned himself Emperor and King of Italy.

Though at peace with him, as well as with the King of France and all the Christian powers, the Republic was nevertheless alarmed by the Lutheran heresy and Moslem dominion. At her gates Suleyman stood up to Charles V and molested Venetian trade.

But Venice was again involved in a naval war when Andrea Doria in command of the Emperor's navy fought the corsair Khaïr Eddin Pasha, captain of the Ottoman fleet.

Doria's indecision, and ill-will caused the Venetians to lose the battle of Treviso, but he claimed the capture of Castel-Nuevo, which the Venetians had meanwhile taken by assault.

The Venetian Senate, realizing that Charles V had only needed allies to spare his own forces, concluded a separate though inglorious peace with Constantinople, which saved the Republic from great danger.

Having learnt by experience, Venice was content to remain a quiet witness of the fierce battle between the Emperor and the King of France, and tried to keep her neutrality even before the progress of the Reformation.

Henceforward, from 1545-1570, under the government of the Doge Piero Landi and his successors, Venice enjoyed a period of calm and prosperity that nations know too rarely.

While trade in wool, carpets, textiles, lace, gilt leather, glass and other products prospered and enriched the city, art enchanted and embellished her.

The huge statues of Mars and Neptune by Jacopo Sansovino were erected during the reign of Francesco Donato. Classical palaces arose along the banks of the Brenta, built by Scamozzi, Palladio and other master architects. The glittering waters of the canals now reflected modern buildings beside the ancient marble palaces with their lace-like aspect, often more Asiatic than European and reminiscent of the Republic's glorious conquests.

The columns of Oriental jasper surmounted by heavy Corinthian capitals supported stucco and gilt ceilings; doors richly chiselled or inlaid with ivory and ebony were surrounded with marvellous carvings, windows were decorated with openwork balconies and hand-rails, parquet floors balanced walls hung with velvets and silks. Around the monumental fireplaces hung paintings by Titian, Tintoretto, Veronese and their lesser though by no means negligeable rivals; everything evoked the splendour of Venetian history.

Emblems, coats of arms, trophies, splendid panoplies and halberds in which gold and silver mingled with steel, helped to decorate the halls.

Furniture became more luxurious. Stamped leather and rich materials were used to cover beds, chairs, coffers and canopies. The festive tables covered with openwork napery were laden with fine gold and silver plate.

A profusion of pearls and jewelry adorned the magnificent clothes and glittered in the light of the sun or of the flickering torches.

Venice, gorged with riches, blazed forth with such patrician luxury, that elegance reached even the poorer houses though on a somewhat reduced scale.

Surprised by the beauty of her monuments, her churches paved with mosaic, her colonnades, her statues, the planning of her gardens, the pomp of her religious cult, the splendour of her processions, her decked-out galleys, the illumination of her gondolas full of music and fireworks, which add fugitive stars to the sky, impressed by all this life of splendid pageantry, by her active industry and trade, the abundance of wines and food of all kinds, and by the busy slave-market, travellers who visited Venice in the middle of the XVIth century proclaimed her to be the most beautiful and opulent city of Christendom.

Richness of material, elegance of form and ornament, precious detail and technical virtuosity characterize the decorative effort of this style, which might have been a parvenu style, if the favour of so much prosperity had not permitted so many great artists to express themselves.

Her economic power had indeed created a new middle class which had to be served, eager to rise, and therefore avid of unbridled luxury. In the City of the Doges everyone was noble by fortune

14

if not by birth; there were more than 6.000 gentlemen in Venice. Next to the nobles of high lineage, a new class was formed of enriched tradesmen, bankers, prelates, who all lived a life of pleasure and good humour.

The gold from all the Mediterranean flowed into this corner of the Adriatic. But the Venetian flag, which flew the seas, had also brought with it Oriental corruption in the wake of her trafficking in slaves, pearls or perfumes.

This elegant and refined life had given birth to an aristocracy of the mind. A taste for Greek studies aroused appreciation of classical beauty. The libraries were filled with rare and precious Latin or Greek manuscripts, richly illuminated, with painted edges, the backs handsomely bound in parchment, so that the shelves might be likened to gardens agreeable to the eye. Printing had developed literary culture and the arts; numerous amateurs and enlightened prelates collected damascened arms, medals, statues, drawings, Flemish, German and Italian pictures. The works of Memling, Albert van Ouwater, Joachim Patinir, Albert Dürer, as well as those of Bellini, Mantegna, Antonello da Messina, Giorgione and Titian were already much sought after.

The nobles were surrounded by artists and men of letters. It was the time when Catherine Cornaro kept her courts of love in the groves of Asolo, when Pietro Bembo wrote his verses, when Aretino, who sat as a parasite at the banquets of princes, became a friend of Titian and found his way to fortune and a death without regrets.

The fleet of galleys with sails billowing in the wind and motley flags flying, rocks in the lagoon, reflecting its lights in the scintillating water at night.

The Arsenal is overflowing with munitions, enough to equip all the ships of the world, according to one traveller.

Peace, economic science and the development of banks supported industry and trade and forged this sovereignty.

A silent and enigmatic government administered an invisible justice and sentenced to death the man who talked too much. This occult power lurked in the shadows of all the splendour enjoyed by the people.

They were not kept away from the princes and nobles who sought popularity. They were charmed by the feasts where they found an illusion of liberty. Fascinated by the splendour of the social round they were flattered by the familiarity of the great ones, who mingled with them on festive occasions. The people took their part in tourneys on the Piazza di San Marco, in princely weddings, during the Carnival and the feast of the Ascension, when every year, sailing on the Bucentaur, surrounded by the nobility at the Port of the Lido, amid the chanting of the clergy and in the presence of foreign ambassadors, the Doge espoused the Adriatic by throwing a golden ring into the sea : " We espouse thee, our sea, to mark our true and perpetual domination over thee. "

Venice had reached that point in splendour which marks the apogee of a civilization, and implies its corruption and decadence. Pleasure and love vie with each other for the hours of this brilliant society, which is about to disintegrate, and amid which Veronese was to live. It provided for him the flashes of life and the brilliant rays, which his palette was to fix with the virtuosity of a genius.

Paolo Veronese became the most fascinating painter of this opulence, and of the gallant nobility which was as expert in business as in the wielding of arms.

In Venice his eyes were filled with the ever changing lights of the sky and the sea : he not only caught the picturesque and dazzling colours on the quays, on the canals shimmering with light, but also the cool pewter grey on the lagoon during a thunderstorm, or the greenish horizons where the line of the water joins that of a cloud perched on the horizon.

Space, air, the sea breezes, the sulphur mists, the green and decomposing streaks of water, all this was painted on his canvases in order that in his large compositions the masses of figures, irradiating their own life in translucent half-tones, might be silhouetted against the receding planes of light in the background. Every time that the hour of colour-symphony in which he revelled struck, Veronese was instinctively able to find in his brush the brownish or violet clouds, the grace of pink sunrises reflected on the classical buildings along the canals or on the lace-like campanili, and the tender and fresh azure of skies, with horizontal flights of birds.

Very delicate shades convey the joyous coming of banners floating in the wind of glory, and express the cry of space through masts and sails and far flung draperies. And, like a gift from Heaven cascading angels shower palm leaves and roses on to the woman chosen and marked by divine desire

When Venice, in a new crusade, was covered with laurels at Lepanto, it was in the caresses and poetry of these light tones that she upheld her victory and the pride of her destiny. Far away on the stormy sea the Turk saw three hundred galleys founder in the disaster.

The deep or acid green of the Murano gardens, the languid rivers which nourished and reflected them, the bright flowers, the sunrays which fondled them with their luminous shafts, distributed their freshness on biblical or mythological scenes, which were enlivened by graceful gestures, such as the swift flight of young girls in swirling silvery draperies wafted by a breeze.

This heroic and gallant mythology evoked by the decorative XVIth century painters, this more demonstrative and gesticulating sentimentality of religious art, was animated by Veronese with a keen observation acquired by constant contact with nature.

When he approached the passionate life of his day and mingled it with his own evangelical interpretation, it was with a practised eye that he put on to his canvas a variety of colours, the play of which had become familiar through his everyday understanding.

The courageous and dissolute young men clad in light armour, who incline their broken lances before the Mother of Christ, the corrupt and pious patrician leaders, the prelates fond of good fare, all entered the reality of his vision with their faces, their movements, the metallic reflections of their armour, the silky folds of their clothes, before being fixed for the future in a picture or a fresco.

Veronese had followed them on the Riva degli Schiavoni, on the bridge of the Rialto, on the water or in gondolas, to the accompaniment of serenades. He had observed them in their processions, their whims, their attitudes, in the shimmering of their rich costumes.

He painted in the style of his masters, but with a personal touch. From Giovanni Bellini he retained the accent of truth, from Pisanello stylization, from Carpaccio the amber warmth and the distinctive tones on material, and the play of light on the surface of architecture, as through arches and colonnades. Mantegna revealed to him the science of construction and classical decoration, Correggio the grace and abandon of beautiful draperies and expressive foreshortening, Bonifazio dei Pitati the quality of colour and the meaning of composition.

Other masters surrounded him, whose works live on the walls of the palaces in the City of the Doges : Titian, bowed by age and glory, Palma il Vecchio painter of noble Venetian ladies, Lorenzo Lotto still able to renew old inventions by a delicate realism and always trying to find himself, above all Tintoretto, whose stormy and tormented thoughts were to lead art towards the sombre evocations of Rembrandt, the fever of Ribera and the tumults of Delacroix.

Certain painters are worth remembering : Jacopo Bassano, Paris Bordone, Il Schiavone, Battista Franco, Horatio Vecelli, Salviati. Drawing their inspiration from the very sources of life, they created definite aesthetic types and isolated them from the crowds with whom they rubbed elbows daily. Fair Venetian ladies sumptuously gowned, elegant cavaliers in close-fitting clothes, senators draped in their purple togas, Turks, Persians or Africans who traded in Circassian slaves, textiles, drugs, spices and exotic animals passed before the eyes of these visionaries in a dream-like pageantry, unfolding a marvellous and continuous spectacle.

Veronese is the glorious emulator of Titian, to whom the master paid public homage. It is towards him that he turned eagerly to idealize his Madonnas or concentrate voluptuousness in the female body, just as he turned to Michelangelo to give force and suppleness to his striking foreshortening. Less vigorous, less dramatic than Titian, less of a sculptor than Michelangelo he knew how to hurl Titans in admirable muscular relaxation. Through life and movement he escaped from false greatness; with his impetuosity he upset the ideal of order and harmony of Raphael or Giulio Romano's lines. This spirit is felt in the architecture and in the balanced masses of a beautiful Venetian landscape.

His compositions are not disturbed by the violent wind which blows Tintoretto's draperies, by the flashes of lightning emanating from the rocks, by the tumult of wings and contrasts of light and shade, which prepare the tradition of the great Spanish painters. The spirit of Albert Dürer and the early Flemings came into Italian painting with Tintoretto, not without some bitterness.

While remaining emotional, Veronese puts more simplicity into his tragic martyrdoms or Calvaries.

While Correggio spiritualizes the flesh and makes it radiate, while Giorgione gives a happy fullness to the flesh and Tintoretto lengthens it shudderingly into a passionate silence, Veronese clothes it in magnificent materials.

In this luxurious *milieu*, where women were so highly appreciated, he succeeded in giving them the worldly expression of patrician Venetian belles.

16

Giorgione, in searching for a style, presented these ladies serenely, bathed in a late afternoon light, in the quiet and russet of autumn, when flesh abandons itself like a mystic savoury fruit.

Titian, who loved them with his sensual passion, made them appear to be awaiting his own desire. With the help of cupids or maidservants, he laid the Venetian belles in a shady landscape or a mysterious alcove, glowing with animal warmth among their draperies and purple cushions, or beneath some heavenly golden rain, queens in a realm of voluptuousness, sure of their offered body, and yet instinctively anxious, listening for the steps of a victor or of some god perhaps, who was about to come. With a gust of wind he freed them of all chastity, revelling in the immodesty of bacchanals, such as Poussin afterwards loved. Sometimes he showed them to us redoubtable and fascinating in the most adorable disarray of clothes, with the lure of a half-veiled breast, their hair falling loose over their shoulders.

Even his Virgins are profane with a terrestial beauty.

His fusion of colours, plastic harmony and fine composition made him one of the most fervent interpretors of the feminine ideal.

Coming like Giorgione from Giovanni Bellini's workshop, Palma il Vecchio created perhaps the most perfect type of Venetian woman, with thick ash-blond hair, triumphant in the splendour of a soft skin, more passive, more abandoned than the type immortalized by Titian.

Tintoretto, the dramatic exponent of light and shade, haunted by Raphael, Titian and Michelangelo, was more intellectual and sought for a higher voluptuousness in his artistic expression. He went in for the opulence of heavy, mature bodies, such as Rubens afterwards remembered.

The patrician ladies painted by Leonardo in Florence are enigmatic, as if wrapped in the mystery of their inner life. A world of dreams surrounds them.

Veronese was to give a splendid and decorative rendering of Venetian women. He did not represent them in warm nudity like Titian, but made them no less redoubtable in gorgeous dresses, sometimes reminiscent of autumn landscapes, equipped with all the artifices of the toilet, — plaited hair twisted round their heads, precious jewels, necklaces, bracelets and dresses that appear to be woven by heavenly hands. They lived the worldly life of their pearls and jewels, in sumptuous palaces, amid the marble columns erected by Palladio to bring back the triumph of classical art, amidst tables laden with gold plate, and servants bedizened like orientals. They have not the pale fairness of Palma Vecchio's women, but their hair reflects the light of autumn leaves, with pearls gleaming amid the coils. He caught their carriage, their elegance, their refined curiosity, their ostentation, the foreshortening of a raised arm, of a breast, of the hand that holds the dress. Outside, the women were followed

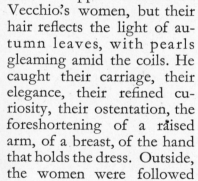

SIMPLICITY. Doge's Palace, Collegio, Venice. Photo Alinari.

by a motley procession, rendered in a feast of colours, wherein their beauty finds its natural background. He puts them in the shadow of foliage, or in luxurious carriages, escorted by servants, black pages bought in the slave market to carry their train, footmen, horses, soldiers, thoroughbred dogs and misshapen dwarfs. He sets them on the banks of a river, where their lovers alight from a boat. Their gestures are those of surprised princesses, making graceful delays to put on their shoes, with puerile suppleness on their flight, to enable their silken clothes to reflect lights like living flesh. Turbans with aiguillettes, light feathers and loose scarves flutter against clumps of trees, the receding line of hills, or peaceful buildings reflected in the mirrored water.

Green skies vie with the warm tones of materials. Silver reflections, born of the shock of cold lights, animate the folds of silk and put into play the magnificent brocades and draperies of Smyrna.

Even the peasant women, clothed in common materials, are endowed with the royal touch of luminous ash greys as though to honour their maternity equally with that of the haughty nobility.

It is like a Persian faerie, the splendour of the Arabian Nights brought by Moslem fellucas, shining in the wonderful canvases of the Museums of Dresden, Lyons, Dijon, in the Prado in Madrid, and the Hermitage in Leningrad : in each case the daughter of the Kings finds the floating destiny of Moses in the Nile.

Charmed by the richness of the subject, which enabled him to transpose into a biblical scene the lordly luxury of his day, the painter exhausted his vision in several picturesque replicas. All show beauty of composition, elegance of attitudes, opulence of detail and a pleasing balance of subject with the background of trees and sky. One cannot help being struck by the ease with which Veronese has varied his interpretation of the scene, though using the same groups and the same figures. In this ability to conceive variously he shows the suppleness of his imagination.

The picture in the Hermitage is really a sketch for the very much larger composition in the Prado. We see how the artist distributed his colours on a restricted scale in order to obtain the decorative effect in the larger picture.

The figures, the sky, the landscape are of secondary importance and only serve to enhance the general effect. The landscape with its mountains and trees, the town and river with the bridge, are calculated to activate their recession and stress the values of the foreground with its dominant colours.

This is an imposing work both in its execution, in its orchestration of tones and its richness, all of which serve to enhance the sumptuous clothes of Pharaoh's daughter.

Is it really possible that Veronese was merely a superficial painter devoid of emotion and intellect ?

He was too well acquainted with the brilliant and picturesque society of his day to consider it otherwise than somewhat disdainfully, though always with the amused eye of a colourist.

We are assured that Paolo was good-looking, gallant and pleasant, though quick tempered, standing on his dignity and never permitting any stain on his honour. His works would prove the contrary to whomsoever who chose to deny it.

V. RELIGIOUS SUBJECTS

Veronese was an exponent of social life and treated his religious subjects without forgetting his taste for modernism; but we are told that he never thought, or went beyond the limits of the outer world.

Nevertheless his religious compositions conceived and executed with a faultless care for stage-effect have a symbolical value, which I hope to point out.

Behind the decorative and easy life of his time, Caliari appears like one of his figures in the *Marriage at Cana*, dressed in brilliant yellow, symbol of inner riches : with eyes cast heavenwards he speaks in a low voice to anyone who cares to listen amid the noise of the feast. If we could hear him he would speak as follows :

In the centre is the head of Jesus and all the lines converge towards it. The nimbus of light surrounding it vibrates more than the others and gives a pure dominant note in which the blue of spirituality, the pink of incarnation, the brilliant yellow of secret gold are allied in a masterly contrast. There is a remote expression on the face of Christ, absorbed in concentration; He appears to take part in the feast and is yet far away from this elegant and motley crowd seated at the table. He has the sweet gravity of one whom a humble servant touches as a power of this world.

The Virgin and the Apostles are seated next to the Son of God at the Divine Table. They are soberly and modestly clad as befits poor relations, who are almost embarrassed to be guests in such splendid surroundings. On the sides (according to a written tradition kept in the Convent of St. George and told to Zanetti) are seated the great ones of this earth in their most sumptuous clothing, ornaments and jewels : the groom on the left at the corner of the table, to whom a little negro is presenting a cup, purports to be Don Alphonso d'Avalos, marquis of Guasto; and the young bride sitting next to him is said to be Eleonora of Austria, Queen of France. Sitting behind her and leaning forward is a madman. Francis I with a curious head dress sits beside him. Among the other guests we find Mary, Queen of England in a yellow gown, Suleyman I (some say Achmet II) Emperor of the Turks, further on Vittoria Colonna, marchioness of Pescara, holding a tooth pick. At the corner of the table the Emperor Charles V is seen in profile, decorated with the order of the Golden Fleece. And beyond are more princes, cardinals, and all are the painter's friends.

The artists themselves give the spiritual concert at God's table — a privilege conferred upon them by the nobility of their art. We find the octogenarian Titian, draped in the purple of passion, moving his bow across the violoncello, and playing the deep note of this symphony to which Palma — or Bassano — mingles the sound of the flute, while Tintoretto, clad in sombre green and Veronese himself, attired in cool colours, add the heavenly tones of the violas.

They are the princes of art. It is their music which draws Christ, indifferent to the gaiety of the guests, gently towards other skies. They participate in the miracle of the Transubstantiation of the wine in jugs, accompanying it by a harmonious cantata ; the miracle of the Word repeats itself.

The *Marriage at Cana* expresses the union of man and divinity. Through the magic of art the colourless water changes into a rare and precious golden wine wherein everything that life contains of vulgar elements is transmuted into a spiritual value. Benedetto Caliari, Paolo's brother raises a cup of this spiritual wine and invites all to partake of it. Wealth, elegance and nobility are gathered round the centre of this composition, with the artists in the foreground. Placed between the spectator and the Presence of God they become the direct intermediaries and invite us to the sacred repast.

The kings, who were admitted only to the side tables, have not been placed there as mere actors. Their presence is not due to a whim on the part of the artist. It is necessary, in order to give significance to the symbol, as well as to enrich the theme of a vast and colourful symphony : faces leaning towards their neighbours, ladies, nobles, charming friends unaware of any miracle; — an indifferent society which is never still, but does not notice what is happening on a higher plane.

Yellows, greens, glistening pinks, purples, blues and the distinguished greys of the brocades and embroideries, worked with a wonderful ability, form the clothes of this chosen society, enraptured with pleasure, and yet unaware of the great secret.

The whole of the mystery is enacted between the marble flagstones and the carved columns, where bedizened slaves are passing to and fro, while full-throated young women lean from the balconies with outstretched arms, glad to see and be seen behind the railings which separate servants from their masters and define the spirit of caste.

From the artistic plane, figuring the group of musicians, Caliari passes to the divine plane, and then on to that of the humble workers, who, unbeknown to themselves, attained saintliness in their daily labour.

In the background a cloudy sky is shimmeringly reflected on the stucco and marble, and a campanile rises towards heaven as a prayer in stone. Higher up three doves inscribe the cipher of the Holy Trinity.

The composition is scientifically disposed in three tiers of alternating light and shadow and the figures detach themselves against the light according to the aesthetics of contrast so dear to the Venetian painters. Thoroughbred dogs help to form the symbolical triangle which encloses the movement and the prodigious virtuosity of colour.

This picture, mentioned as a marvel by Vasari in the Life of Michele Sammichele, was a commission of the Benedictines of San Giorgio Maggiore, the island opposite the Piazzetta, to decorate the hall of their convent, rebuilt by Palladio. This hall was spacious, light and well vaulted. The Fathers first asked Veronese to paint a fresco above the door. He painted two angels inviting silence. The monks were satisfied with his work and drew up an agreement on the 6th of June 1562 which is still in the archives of the convent; according to it Veronese agreed to paint his great masterpiece for the sum of 324 gold ducats in addition to his board, the cost of paints and the gift of a keg of wine. The painting was completed on the 8th September 1563, as agreed.

In 1799 Napoleon brought it to France after his Italian campaign. Removed from the setting for which it was intended, the picture was transported to the Louvre in Paris. In 1815 it was claimed by the Austrian Government, but owing to the difficulties and dangers of transport it was exchanged for a canvas of Lebrun, engraved by Poilly, representing *Christ in the House of Simon the Pharisee* and Veronese's masterpiece remained in the Louvre.

Paolo treated the subject several times. The Brera Gallery, Milan, has a canvas of smaller size, which should not be mistaken for the one in the Louvre. There is also a *Marriage at Cana* in the Prado, Madrid, bought by Philip IV at the sale of Charles I's Collection; it was sent to the Escorial, and represents ten people seated in a sumptuous guest-chamber opening on to a garden, Jesus and Mary occupying the centre of the semi-circular table, served by eight well dressed attendants.

The *Marriage at Cana* consecrated the glory of Veronese. He was highly esteemed by all the great contemporary painters of Venice. Titian kissed him one day in the street and the morose Tintoretto found elegant words to praise his rival.

His fame spread and brought him numerous commissions from religious communities, and he was much in demand for the decoration of churches and convents.

Father Torlioni, his first patron, commissioned him to paint the *Leper's Feast* for the Convent of St. Sebastian. Three years later he painted a *Feast in the House of Levi* on one of the walls of the refectory in the Dominican Convent of St. John and Saint Paul; this was his third feast. It is now in the Accademia delle Belle Arte in Venice and combines pageantry with all the qualities that made him famous. We see pages playing on the steps of a magnificent palace, negroes carrying ewers, and as usual, Venetian ladies in their stiff, spreading dresses. Veronese displayed all the resources of his palette.

It has been remarked that all this was hardly of a nature to sanctify the Dominican's thoughts; yet the painter had several times proved his disinterestedness.

The fourth Lord's Supper known as *Jesus in the House of Simon the Pharisee* was painted for the refectory of the Servites and is in the Louvre. It presents a cold sobriety in contrast to the gaiety of the *Marriage at Cana*. The guests are humbler. A feeling of family devotion hovers over the scene, where the Magdalen wipes the Saviour's feet with her golden tresses. It cannot be said that the best was not put out to receive the Master. The richness of the tablecloth proves the contrary, but the table is laid without any ostentation. Christ is nearer to these middle-class men, whose life slips by uneventfully in a peace which is allied to sanctity. He converses with them simply. Magdalen's humility is expressed in an adorable smile, and happiness radiates from her lowered head.

Purity emanates from the luminous table-cloth, from the white linen and dresses. The attenuated, passionless colouring, the gentle light on the town houses, bathed in a blue-grey atmosphere bespeak of quiet hearts, while the cool depths of the sky traversed by angels, opens on to an immense green vista.

Many people may object and ask if the painter really intended all this to appear. Cannot we read his works? And is not an artist worth everything we can extract from him?

This picture was painted between 1570-1575 for the refectory of the Servites in Venice, and was presented to Louis XIV in 1665 by the Venetian Republic. It first hung in the Galerie d'Apollon and later in the reign of Louis XV was taken to Versailles and placed in the Salon of Hercules.

Let us now turn to another picture of the same period, signed in golden letters, which is now the property of the Louvre: *Christ at Emmaus*.

Here Christ is seen calling down the blessing of the Father on the simple and hospitable table with pilgrims seated round it. Tradition has it that Veronese depicted himself and his family. But a more authentic source prefers to consider the pilgrims as the family of the donor.

In the series of sacred feasts we must mention *Jesus in the House of Simon the Pharisee* in the Brera Gallery, Milan. Another picture of the same subject hangs in the Pinacoteca in Turin. The *Feast in the House of Levi* is in the Accademia, Venice and lastly a *Supper of St. Gregory the Great* decorates the walls of the Convent of Monte Berico, Vicenza.

Any subject painted by several artists enables us to form an opinion as to the value of their individual conception and interpretation. Let us compare the banquets of Veronese with those of other masters.

His opulence and grandeur contrasts with the vivid light effects and the austerity of Tintoretto.

In his *Last Supper* painted for San Giorgio Maggiore, Venice, Tintoretto used all his visionary gifts. The adorable face of Christ radiates light, reflected on the faces of the guests who are seated at a simple trestle-table covered with a rough cloth and set with modest plate; he stirs up so much divine fervour that one feels the miracle is indeed taking place.

A storm of light and shade emanates from Tintoretto's violence. Veronese bathes the head of Christ and the passionless features of the apostles in a holy atmosphere, palpitating with spiritual serenity. Quiet hearts beat peacefully in the limpid air.

Thus we can measure the distance that separates two exceptionally gifted artists, who lived at the same time and who sought to express themselves in the same language, but with a totally different accent; and we can estimate the various resources which may be obtained from the common treasure of art.

The *Marriage at Cana* painted for the Church of the Salute in Venice, reveals a Tintoretto who had not made full use of his genius; but the striking contrast of light and shade and the concave composition, in the manner of Veronese, but all gathered under one imperious diagonal again shows us what separates the two masters.

Jacopo Bassano, coming after them, was more humble and used a more familiar realism. His *Marriage at Cana* in the Louvre, does not take us into the houses of the great, but into the dwelling of some well-to-do landowner, who has given of his best. The saintly conversation continues during the coming and going of the servants. A child is twanging the chords of an instrument, which the musicians have left behind. They are not in the picture, but have placed their violas and flutes on the ground during the interval. Animals are taking part in the feast, which lacks no produce from field or stream.

Veronese's noble vision is contrasted with this popular conception, full of ingenious foreshortening.

It is perhaps opportune in this synthesis to mention Leonardo's famous *Last Supper* painted for the refectory of Santa Maria della Grazie, where one distinguishes even more clearly the divergence of interpretation by another more highly gifted artist.

Here the values are all austere and symbolical. The drama is expressed by the groups, by the attitudes and gestures, with an inner animation and with the purely intellectual simplicity of a genius who mingles the classical spirit with emancipated modern values perfectly harmoniously.

*

Undoubtedly, Veronese was not merely a painter in love with the brilliant pageantry of Venetian life, which spread itself before his eyes and which he rendered on canvas in such a masterly fashion; he was too clever not to feel the shock to sentiment created by the dry feeling of Tintoretto, who expressed himself in mysterious and disturbing harmonies.

The psychological depth of his rivals, Tintoretto and Titian, could not have escaped Veronese. It is probably difficult to concentrate pictorial emotion in very large paintings. In his work it is somewhat crushed by the sumptuous setting.

He nevertheless excelled in the art of rendering the tragedy of suffering as well as the spectacle of joy, or serenity. Witness his splendid *Calvary* in the Louvre.

On a livid green sky receding to a light horizon, through fugitive pale clouds, Christ stands out on the Cross, not in a twisted agony but relaxed as in death. The bodies of the two thieves are deeper in tone and set off the body of Christ. His face stands out light against the mass of dark hair, surrounded by a luminous halo.

Disciples, holy women and soldiers attending to the fainting Virgin are grouped at the foot of the Cross. They are painted in a minor key of violet, green and dark red and the low tones emphasize the Virgin's palor and the luminous body of the Redeemer.

The holiness of the group expresses itself in the yellow cloak of the pious woman praying; the vibration of her erect figure supports the whole composition, arranged diagonally against one of the most beautiful backgrounds of sky in the whole of Italian painting. In the distance, people are gathering on the roads leading to the city, which sleeps in a limpid blue.

Caliari's religious subjects are in all the museums of Europe. In the Prado at Madrid is one of them representing *Jesus among the Doctors*, which formed part of the collection belonging to Charles II. The Son of God is speaking from a pulpit of a beautiful Renaissance temple. At the back near the doorway is the weeping Virgin accompanied by St. Joseph looking for the lost divine Child. The celebrated picture of *Jesus and the Centurion* is also in the Prado. Here Veronese has illustrated a passage from the Gospel of St. Matthew. It hung originally in the Escorial, having been sent there by Philip IV.

The Centurion clad in armour is kneeling before the Saviour on the marble pavement of a sumptuous building. Two soldiers with halberds are leaning forward to support their chief while a richly attired page holds his helmet. Between the columns more soldiers gaze at the scene. A splendid building is seen in the background and above it one of those broad and distant skies that the painter excels in depicting; another version of the same subject, but differently treated also belongs to the Prado.

The *Pietà* in the Hermitage in Leningrad reveals yet another aspect of the spiritual way in which Veronese conceived a religious subject.

The body of Christ is lying on a stone covered by a shroud. From behind the Mater Dolorosa bends forward in a touching attitude contemplating the dear agonised face. An angel holds her hand in one of his and with the other raises the arms of Christ, which are still stiff from the Crucifixion.

The deliberate simplicity of effect contrasts with Veronese's usual elaboration. The group of three figures stands out not against a distant landscape but on a dark background with a masterful composition and with astonishing foreshortening.

Only the head and shoulders of the Virgin appear. The attitude of the other people, whose faces are gradated in light and shadow emphasize the simplicity of the scene. The effective light, the masterly gradation of colour take the place of decoration and accessories.

Veronese portrayed pain with inspired sobriety and dramatic quality and opposed it to the divine calm attained in death after untold torture.

Yet another picture shows what his art could reach without any ostentation. The magnificent *Vision of St. Helena* is the pride of the National Gallery. She is represented sleeping with her elbow resting on a wide parapet. She is clothed in splendid draperies, and the delicacy, the peculiar quality of Veronese's colours, his art of clothing his figures compel our admiration. Angels appear in the young woman's dream bringing her the gift of the Cross to be adored in the silence of her sleep.

The composition of this picture sets off the distribution of light and shade according to the Venetian formula, a quarter of shadow, a quarter of light and the rest in half tones or against the light.

The gleam of the draperies, which Rubens tried to equal in a more violent effect, was obtained easily by silvery streams. By this means Veronese confers the royalty of light upon his figures.

SECULAR PAINTINGS.

The display of luxury in Veronese's sacred scenes served as a pretext for the intervention of the Inquisition; they must have noted the very unorthodox symbolism in his pictures. We know how Veronese defended himself, when he was accused of having treated a religious subject too lightly. The records of the investigation have been preserved and were published by A. Baschet and they give us a very good idea of the suspicions which could at the time cramp an artist's expression.

It is very likely that the painter was obliged to moderate his imagination after such a solemn warning.

He must have found the occasion to revenge himself, when he was commissioned in 1575 to decorate the Palace of the Doges, at the pressing invitation of the Signoria of Venice.

Veronese treated the profane subjects with delight, as he was at ease within the broader limits.

THE ADORATION OF THE MAGI. Library of the École des Beaux-Arts, Paris. Photo Giraudon.

Mythology furnished subjects wherein his gifts expressed themselves more readily than in some of his religious compositions. Thus he made his sacrifice to the humanism of the Renaissance.

The joy of colour brings Veronese irresistibly towards *Parnassus*, Mantegna's masterpiece in the Louvre, where the Muses dance before Apollo to the sound of sacred incantations with the freshness of immortal youth.

The religious pictures were well suited to the architectural setting for which they were designed, but did not correspond to monastic ideas; the mythological subjects, on the other hand, were equally well adapted to the beautiful classical buildings which Palladio, Sansovino, Longhena, Alessandro Vittoria, Antonio da Ponte, Camozzi and so many others erected, and which were the pride of Venice; and they were in accord with the gallant life of the day.

We may rightly say that Veronese's rendering of picturesque anecdote, the gestures of his figures, the luxury of attire and architecture are so pleasing to the eye, that nothing remains to satisfy the heart.

He solves the problem of allegory by clever foreshortening, by scientific distribution of light, by the spatial splendour of heavenly blues, and the modelling of forms in silhouette.

We have seen that occasionally Veronese was able to raise himself to a spiritual plane and give a deep significance to his work. In his profane pictures he only sought to please. A suggestion of colour was always a successful element. He must have taken great precautions to maintain the freshness of his pigments. Unlike those of Leonardo, his colours have endured throughout the centuries.

As a result of a fire which occured in 1574 in the upper storeys of the Doges' Palace, Caliari was commissioned to commemorate the unforgettable *Victory of Lepanto* which accomplished the defeat of the Turks. He represented Venice enthroned between Justice and Peace, the former holding a sword, the latter an olive branch. In a complex symbol, well adapted to the setting, he painted a series of panels with virtues on the ceiling, and over the throne the Doge Sebastian Veniero between St. Mark

23

and Saint Justina with the proveditor Agostino Barbarigo behind them, holding the flag of the Republic. Above the routed Moslem fleet, among a bevy of angels, Christ soars holding the globe and blessing the victors.

Another fire in 1577 destroyed the long series of masterpieces of Venetian art from Gentile da Fabriano and Pisanello to the Bellinis, Titian and Veronese.

The Signoria wished to restore the vast decoration. Two noble scholars Jacopo Marcello and Jacopo Contarini were entrusted with this work. The more important part, the decoration of the ceiling in the Hall of the Grand Council fell to Veronese. The *Apotheosis of Venice* is a vast synthesis, concentrating all his science of aerial composition, his technique in perspective and foreshortening, his taste for elegant suspended architecture, his delight in refined and picturesque luxury, his love of children, of dogs and of horses. It is the consummate art of a magician, full of joy, poetry and symbols.

In the foreground the oval concentrates a tumultuous mass of soldiers, horses and dogs in the street; then on the balcony of a sumptuous palace, with expressive horizontal parallels like the waters of the lagoon, parades all the splendour and nobility of Venice, — gallant ladies and young girls. Venice is enthroned above, seated on a cloud, which seems caught and held by two twisted columns. A large woman in the style of Palma, is clothed in royal purple and holds a sceptre. An angel from heaven is about to place a crown on her head, while the clarion of Fame carries the echo of her greatness to the four winds of the sky.

The proud city of the Adriatic had found her most opulent glorifier.

Caliari completed the splendid history of his adopted city with the celebration of her military triumphs. Though his virtuosity permitted him to treat any subject with credit he was never really a painter of battle scenes.

His exceptional gifts for composition and execution are to be found in the *Defense of Smyrna*, the *Victory over the Turks*, the *Conquest of Scutari* by the Doge Loredano, the *Victorious Return of Contarini* after the victory at Chioggia, and the *Departure of Pope Alexander III's envoys for Pavia*.

In these works the painter's brilliant qualities were somewhat limited by the uncongenial subjects. It is probable that they were painted with the aid of his pupils.

*
* *

In the gallant mythology of Veronese we find all the gaiety, the ease and the freshness of the school of Parma. Corregio had already enthralled his age with his smiling creations. He stretched luminous bodies beneath trees, he made nudity radiate, and heavenly children hover like butterflies; he knew how to drape material, stylise the superhuman type by reducing the head, by lengthening the limbs to represent demi-gods or heroes.

Veronese was charmed by his grace and youthful joy and dipped his brush into the same source of inspiration. How readily he too creased materials and displayed brocades, such as Carpaccio had used, to clothe his goddesses as if they were great ladies. The *Rape of Europa* in the ducal Palace, Venice, is one of the best examples of the Correggian ease, witty, slightly frivolous, yet remaining chaste.

A tenderly naïve Europa seats herself on the bull, one breast emerging from the many folds of her garment. Her handmaidens, with graceful movements, help the beautiful Phœnician to mount the divine animal crowned with roses, and cupids holding wreaths flutter in the trees; in the distance a murmuring sea continues the poetry of this faerie towards a distant horizon.

The colours of the flesh and the materials are in harmonious tones of pink, yellow and mauve with the bluish foliage and golden sky as a background.

We are far from the warm and sensual art of Giorgione and Titian; we are at the dawn of a new aesthetic, which was to inspire the XVIIIth century. These graceful lines were to be followed in France by Boucher, Lemoyne, and de Troy.

In a picture in the Prado Veronese has represented Venus and Adonis. The beautiful hunter is asleep with his head resting on the goddess's lap, his left hand lying on his breast, the right one on the horn strapped to his side. Venus, half nude and slightly leaning forwards, shields the sleeper from the bright light. A dog lies at their feet, and another is being restrained by Cupid, lest its barking might waken the master and urge him to rise and leave.

The same qualities are seen in a *Dying Cleopatra* in the Royal Gallery in Cassel.

The attribution of this picture has often been contested. For a long time it was thought to be by

Titian. Some experts have maintained that it was by Cesare Vecellio, a brother of the Master of Cadore. But Bode ascribes it to Veronese, and his opinion seems nearer the truth.

There was some doubt as to the subject as well as the artist's name, a woman dying from a snake-bite could hardly wear such a beautiful smile, and an amateur had the serpent painted over. Subsequently, when the picture was cleaned the serpent re-appeared and was thought to be an addition. At one time the picture was supposed to be *Ariadne* abandoned at Naxos, dreaming of her deliverer.

The landscape represents a sea, with ships and soldiers disembarking. In all respects this picture is worthy of Veronese's brush.

When Caliari tries his hand at allegory he again gives proof of his prodigious imagination, whether he defies the four elements, or celebrates the four seasons in a symbolical manner, reviving the spirit of Ovid. The mother of Cupids appears as a vision of spring, among roses and airy winged children, surrounded by young women radiating light and youth.

Elsewhere, semi-divine and semi-agrestic figures disport themselves in rustic groups under the triumphant eye of a god during the haymaking and grape-gathering seasons.

*
* *

When Veronese painted portraits he endeavoured to find more in his models than mere external reflexions, I mean he tried to portray the essential face with subtle psychological values.

Caliari excelled at interpreting the distinction of high breeding. But was he ever truly a portrait painter ? I am inclined to think that he was chiefly pre-occupied with his vast compositions. When he peopled them with faces of his contemporaries he only retained the variety of type and attitudes to obtain contrasts and accents depending on the requirements of his compositions. He was rarely interested in resemblance.

In the *Marriage at Cana* we undoubtedly have fairly good likenesses of Titian, Tintoretto, Bassano, Benedetto Caliari and Veronese himself, because the artist wanted to magnify himself among his peers at God's Table. But are we right in recognising the important personages that Zanetti has described ?

Caliari only seems to have sought the necessary elements to accompany his theme and grant magnificence to the Kings, princes and patricians at this luxurious feast. Let us continue to see with charmed eyes the celebrated personalities in this web of moving colour, but refrain from seeking too much likeness in this pageant.

The faces of the Pilgrims of Emmaus seem nearer to living reality. We are again assured that Veronese represented himself with all his family here. On the right, stands a woman holding a baby in her arms, next to her are two young girls and two sons, one of whom seems timid and is hiding in the folds of her dress, while the other is kneeling and holding a spaniel.

In the foreground two little girls clad in brocade are patting a dog. We are certainly looking at a religious subject. But is it not at the same time one which portrays the family of the donor ? It is unlikely that Veronese sought to express much character in the faces, which were only part of the whole composition. Yet the children's portraits are adorable ! They seem full of childish charm : some attentive, already serious, while the others are happy and carefree, naïvely playful and full of fun. What a charming memory one carries away of the two little girls in the foreground !

Ghirlandaio gives us the sensation of freshness in a child's face, Raphael models fat bambini and instinctively gives them spontaneity and charming grace; Corregio's children lightly flutter in audacious foreshortening.

Following his example, Veronese depicts children who seem to plunge from any heights with consummate art. Even in his allegorical phantasies they are the children of a fine painter who gives them the kiss of light.

But the artist draws his child from the azure heavens to fondle it in the family circle. He makes an enchanting creature of it, clothing it sumptuously like a precious doll full of inexplicable movements, reflections and playful charm. He emphasizes its joy of living, its reactions similar to those of a young animal, and then by degrees, as the child grows older he transforms it into a being eager for knowledge, full of curiosity, attention and the wish to understand and share the life of grown-ups.

That is how Veronese became one of the best painters of children.

Though he may not always retain psychological values, Veronese knows how to exalt the charm and attraction of his models. He excels in making a beautiful woman radiate grace in drawing

25

a flush to the skin and in making her a centre towards which all desires and wishes of happiness appear to converge. The uncontested proof is the portrait of *La Belle Nani* in the Louvre; she is as fresh as a rose, whose bloom cannot be destroyed by a stormy night and who comes towards us in all the magic of her youth, the prestige of a supple and harmonious body discernable beneath the rich material. The quality of her velvety skin and wonderful eyes make her fascinating and desirable, perhaps in spite of herself. Her jewels and sumptuous clothes lose their importance beside the attraction of her face.

In this picture, the art of the portrait painter is particularly noticeable. For a moment we forget about other interpretors of the feminine ideal : the divine and impassive profiles of Ghirlandaio, the Madonnas and fine psychological portraits of Raphael, the beautiful tresses of Palma Vecchio, the mysterious depth of Leonardo and the concentrated silence of Titian.

Veronese is certainly suggestive in his quality, his subtle distinction which is colder and more spiritual. I should say he holds us by his mind rather than by the senses and arouses more intellectual demands.

VII. THE POETRY OF VERONESE. HIS DRAWINGS

Veronese's marvellous technique establishes him as the great decorator of the XVIth century in Italy and as one of the finest painters of all times. He evokes visions before which the mind hesitates and is suddenly raised and carried by a mysterious wave towards heights, where art becomes an expression of metaphysics blended with religion.

No one has succeeded so completely in producing an intoxicating effect by the magic use of colour alone.

Veronese did not brutally sweep away the frames of classical reason. The art of Mantegna, Giovanni Bellini, Giorgione and Titian assigned him certain limits which he sometimes transcended, but more often he juggled with them very adroitly, by introducing active light and life. This virtuoso created a symphony of colour without overstepping the bounds laid down for his work.

He follows the Venetian practice of producing a monochrome underpainting in tempera, covered with oil glazes, sufficiently transparent to show the grisaille underneath. Like his predecessors, Veronese begins by roughly sketching his forms and movements. His lines are firm and sure. Then he outlines them in ocre, and then models vigorously in broad progressive strokes.

Look at the head of the dog in the centre foreground of the *Marriage at Cana* and you will get a precise idea of his solid, brilliant technique, which inspired Rubens and Delacroix.

Already Titian, breaking with tradition, had merged his contours by superimposing them in order to reduce the contrast of tones. Veronese used this manner freely. By emphasizing the drawing and values and by his sense of foreshortening, he felt at ease in his vast compositions.

The usual disposition of his Suppers induced him to adopt a concave composition. The colours mount gradually in a scale of tones from the outside towards the most distant central point.

In order to complete the hollow thus obtained, the painter placed a dominant movement in the centre of the foreground. This takes us away from Titian's convex composition and the pyramid of Raphael. Caliari excels in the art of placing masses on their right plane without recourse to the subterfuge of violent oppositions.

He never sought the concentrated effect of Titian and Tintoretto. His chiaroscuro remains luminous and light. His pictures are not suddenly torn by a devouring depth of shadow which both painters made use of to strengthen their effects. While they painted light figures against brown tones Veronese modelled in full light.

His figures are bathed in a limpid atmosphere which envelopes and penetrates them, gives them an airy ease, free gestures, and lends a harmonious transparency to the whole picture. The painter creates a vast symphony supported by connected contrasts in which the active and subordinate values are all joined into an incomparable harmony.

In this play of exact relations we find the quick union between the brain which conceived and the hand which executed as promptly as lightning. It is the sign of great artists.

This limpid airy web of colour never struggles against the receding sky. Caliari knows how to establish true relations by carefully treating the architectural perspectives which give majesty, grandeur and background.

ST. ANDREW.
Albertina, Vienna. Photo Braun & Cie.

Veronese can always bear the brilliant comparison with Raphael and Titian, even when he creates slow and distinguished harmonies.

Look at the marvellous *Esther before Ahasuerus* in the Salon Carré in the Louvre : the picture is bathed in luminous greeny-yellow tones, which do not fade before the tragic *Entombment* by Titian or the enveloping charm of Raphael's *Holy Family*.

His eloquence, his light grisaille do not give way before the warm density of the one, or the perfection of the other. He imposes his spiritual, luminous and cold effect. One is disconcerted by the elegance of his style and the magic of his execution. A small number of masterpieces give that richness of harmony, that luminosity so ably distributed, that measured scientific effect which is the expression of an artistic will, by very simple means. By working in a slow measure, with colours that one would seek elsewhere in vain, the painter effected a sensation of royalty that is unforgettable if only for its privilege of caressing light in a luminous interior.

The same qualities in a lesser degree can be seen in the open-air feeling of *Suzanna and the Elders*. In a sober setting, the splendid garments of the bather and the semi-nudity of her fair living flesh harmonise with the inertia of the smooth stones and with the play of the leaves, patterned in relation to the cold greyness of the sky, the cloudy expanse of which accords with the troubled desire of the elders.

In his elegant vision Caliari tempers the warm oriental symphony that Gentile Bellini and Carpaccio first revealed to Venice.

He remains a Veronese though he becomes a Venetian. To the golden warmth which is concentrated in Titian's art, both sensual and controlled, he opposes cold lights. One is pleased to discover in him some of the spirituality and feeling which constitute the charm of certain Florentines.

His brush leaves a silvery phosphorescent trail on the transparent greens, on the cold blues supporting the whites, emphasizing the yellows with madders and, if necessary, with streaks of bright red and green. He knows how to mingle them with dark browns and ochres into a superior orchestration, while leaving the greys, violets, pinks and lilacs, the nonchalance of melancholy tones dying away, to be remembered by Whistler.

It is due to this palette that the artist was able to substitute the pale, elegant aristocratic figures who announce Van Dyck for the ruddy, sanguine, sunburnt men or the warm and golden women of Titian.

*
* *

Less careful than Titian in his still life, Veronese is better at rendering animals.

Titian who had a passionate love for the female form and was interested in the psychology of masculine faces seems to have cared little for animals. When he had to introduce a dog, a sheep, a rabbit or a dove into his composition he used the subterfuge of style. Veronese is more instinctive in his attitude. He expresses the distinction of a thoroughbred dog, which lives round the tables of the nobility and contrasts it with the loyal mongrel issued from a chance crossbreed that plays with the children in modest interiors. He loves horses for their nobility and their fugue, which suits his brush and he knows how to make them rear between gripping knees or in the tumult of battles.

His landscapes are less analytic than Giorgione's or Titian's, but are more broadly treated and more decorative in effect.

He is above all a painter of space, with gradated blue-green skies, and moving clouds receding towards a cold luminous horizon. They are lighter and more subtle than Titian's skies, nor are they accentuated with shadowy depths, violence and torment, as are the later skies of Annibale Carracci.

*
* *

The secret of a painter's prestige lies in the magic of colour, in his beautiful handling, but the lightness of his hand may be seen in his drawings. They reveal in their bareness the first qualities of inspiration, the intuitive powers of research and invention, the powers of composition, expression and, if need be, of picturesque arrangement.

A certain number of drawings by Veronese have survived; some are in pen and wash, others in pen and ink heightened with white, others in pen and ink and black chalk with washes of bistre, or heightened with white on grey-blue paper, and others again in pen and water-colour.

TWO KNIGHTS. Musée de Condé, Chantilly. Photo Giraudon.

Firm and dignified in their composition, they occasionally remind one of the antique in the beauty and grace of the faces, the proud carriage, the noble gestures, and the clever disposition of the draperies.

There is a series of eighteen in the Louvre, which are all interesting in their diverse execution. The sketches on grey paper heightened with gouache give an unforgettable impression of freshness in the soft silvery colour, which we find in most of the master's work. The solidity of composition in these drawings, the excellent spacing and careful execution of every detail show the artist's concern to assure a minute preparation for the final picture. Nothing was left to chance or to last minute improvisation.

After transferring the precise and well-constructed linear design on to canvas, Veronese would sketch in the tones, and then his brush would add the enchantment of colour with his customary virtuosity.

His work often reflects the style of Correggio and Parmigiano. Here a young woman holds a clock with an allegorical gesture, and the details of her drapery are rendered with so much elegance and subtlety that the simplest materials appear sumptuous; there a Virgin bends down in a familiar gesture to present her divine Child to St. Francis of Assisi; elsewhere five angels support a terrestial globe upon which Jesus is standing. Religious subjects such as the *Adoration of the Magi* and the *Assumption* figure among the drawings as well as mythological subjects and allegories.

A man and a child standing attract our attention by the natural simplicity of their attitude; and the head of a negro in black and red chalk, heightened with white, shows the delight with which Veronese studied various types.

29

In the British Museum there is a beautiful *Rest on the Flight into Egypt* in silvery white and grey on greenish prepared paper and a *Holy Family* in chalk and bistre on blue-grey paper. These highly finished drawings contrast with a number of slight pen sketches — first ideas for compositions showing how carefully Veronese planned the design of his large altar-pieces.

VIII.   THE PUPILS OF VERONESE AND HIS INFLUENCE

Veronese's rich and varied work influenced a number of painters.

We have already mentioned Paolo's brother Benedetto Caliari, who was born in 1538 and died in 1598; he helped his brother and together with his nephews completed those pictures which Veronese had left unfinished. He imitated the master's style very successfully in the pictures he painted alone.

Veronese had two sons. One Carlo or Carletto, was born in 1572 and died in 1596, at the age of 24; he studied under his father and under Jacopo Bassano, collaborated with the former and himself produced some remarkable work.

His brother Gabriele gave up painting after the deaths of his uncle and brother and died of the plague in Venice in 1631, at the age of 63.

Caliari's principal followers were Parrasio Michele, Luigi Benfatto known as dal Friso, a nephew of Paolo's, Matteo Verona, Luigi's son-in-law, Michelangio Aliprando, Francesco Montemazzano, Sigismonde Scarsella da Ferrara, father of Scarsellino and above all Battista Zelotti, his early collaborator.

Annibale Carracci, Pietro da Cortona, Roselli, Turchi, Crespi, each in turn among many others closely imitated the manner of Paolo. Through Veronese the art of Mantegna and of the Bellini reaches to Tiepolo, a still more luminous painter of a maritime Venice, whose splendour in the XVIIIth century was evaporating.

Rubens, the great Fleming, who learnt so much from the Italians, was also inspired by the great decorator's art.

It was from Caliari that Poussin and Claude Lorrain learnt about the architectural value of monuments in a landscape, and Lebrun found the secret of large compositions.

Veronese, after having influenced the French XVIIth century, prepared the way for the XVIIIth century pictures of *Fêtes galantes*, and mythological voluptuousness. Watteau's florid dresses were not woven by fairies, but by the Italian looms of Veronese; we recognise the Venetian's bold brush in the hands of De Troy, Lemoine, Boucher, in the spirited technique of Fragonard, in Greuze's broad manner and in the lightning stroke of Delacroix.

The light harmonies of grey and ash-green of Titian's rival haunted Whistler and Turner, and vibrated in the trembling silvery tones of Corot.

Veronese died on the 19th of April 1588. He lies in Venice, beneath a simple stone in the Church of St. Sebastian where he had worked so much. His fortune, which was estimated three years before his death by the fiscal assessment, consisted of small properties in Castelfranco and in Santa Maria in Porto and of six thousand sequins in the bank.

Veronese had declined Phillip II's offer to go and decorate the Escorial. It was a noble example of disinterestedness. This contempt for material advantage was doubtless an indication of inner riches and of the prodigality which dispensed so many happy gifts to astonish and fascinate others.

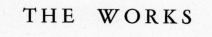

THE WORKS

PORTRAIT OF A YOUNG WOMAN

Musée du Louvre, Paris
Photo Hyperion

SELF-PORTRAIT

Uffizi, Florence
Photo Alinari

34

PORTRAIT OF DANIELE BARBARO
Pitti, Florence
Photo Alinari

PORTRAIT OF DANIELE BARBARO
Pinacothek, Dresden
Photo Alinari

PORTRAIT OF PACIO GUARIENTI

Museo Civico, Verona
Photo Alinari

MADONNA WITH THE CUCCINA FAMILY

Pinacothek, Dresden
Photo Braun et Cte

THE ADORATION OF THE MAGI

Pinacothek, Dresden
Photo Braun et C\ie

MADONNA WITH THE CUCCINA FAMILY (Detail of Pl. 38)
Pinacothek, Dresden
Photo Braun et C¹ᵉ

THE ANNUNCIATION
Chapter Rooms, Escurial, Madrid
Photo Anderson

42

THE MARRIAGE AT CANA (Detail of Pl. 71)

Musée du Louvre, Paris
Photo Hyperion

THE ANNUNCIATION
Academy, Venice
Photo Alinari

THE ARCHANGEL OF THE ANNUNCIATION (Detail)

Academy, Venice
Photo Braun et Cⁱᵉ

THE VIRGIN OF THE ANNUNCIATION (Detail)
Academy, Venice
Photo Alinari

THE ADORATION OF THE MAGI

Academy, Venice
Photo Alinari

THE VIRGIN AND CHILD IN GLORY WITH SAINTS
Academy, Venice
Photo Alinari

THE HOLY FAMILY
Musée du Louvre, Paris
Phot. Arch. Phot. d'Art et d'Hist.

THE HOLY FAMILY
Musée du Louvre, Paris
Photo Hyperion

THE VIRGIN AND CHILD WITH ST. ANTHONY

San Sebastiano, Venice
Photo Alinari

THE HOLY FAMILY WITH ST. BARBARA
Uffizi, Florence·
Photo Alinari

THE HOLY FAMILY WITH ANGELS MAKING MUSIC
Drawing. Musée du Louvre, Paris
Photo Giraudon

THE REST ON THE FLIGHT INTO EGYPT

Drawing. British Museum
Photo Braun et Cie

THE MARRIAGE OF ST. CATHERINE (Detail of Pl. 56)
S. Caterina, Venice
Photo Alinari

THE MARRIAGE OF ST. CATHERINE (Detail of Pl. 56)
S. Caterina, Venice
Photo Alinari

THE MARRIAGE OF ST. CATHERINE

S. Caterina, Venice
Photo Alinari

THE MARRIAGE OF ST. CATHERINE
Museum of Montpellier
Photo Hyperion

THE MARRIAGE OF ST. CATHERINE

Antoine Orliac Collection, Paris
Photo P. Delbo

JESUS AMONG THE DOCTORS

Prado, Madrid
Photo Anderson

59

CHRIST AND THE CENTURION

Pinacothek, Dresden
Photo Braun et Cie

CHRIST AND THE CENTURION
Prado, Madrid
Photo Anderson

HISTORICAL SCENE
Drawing. British Museum
Photo Braun et Cᵗᵉ

Paulo Veronese.

HEAD OF A MAN

Drawing. British Museum
Photo Braun et Cⁱᵉ

ST. JOHN IN THE WILDERNESS

Villa Borghese, Rome
Photo Alinari

64

THE BAPTISM OF CHRIST
Pitti, Florence
Photo Hyperion

THE MARRIAGE AT CANA
Drawing. Weimar Museum
Photo Braun et Cie

THE MARRIAGE AT CANA (Detail of Pl. 67)
Pinacothek, Dresden
Photo Alinari

THE MARRIAGE AT CANA

Prado, Madrid

Photo Anderson

THE MARRIAGE AT CANA

Musée du Louvre, Paris
Photo Braun et Cⁱᵉ

71

THE MARRIAGE AT CANA (Detail of Pl. 71)

Musée du Louvre, Paris

Photo Braun et Cⁱᵉ

THE MARRIAGE AT CANA (Detail of Pl. 71)

Musée du Louvre, Paris
Photo Hyperion

THE MARRIAGE AT CANA (Detail of Pl. 71)
Musée du Louvre, Paris
Photo Alinari

THE MARRIAGE AT CANA (Detail of Pl. 71)
Musée du Louvre, Paris
Photo Alinari

THE FEAST IN THE HOUSE OF SIMON THE PHARISEE

Musée du Louvre, Paris
Photo Arch. Phot. d'Art et d'Hist.

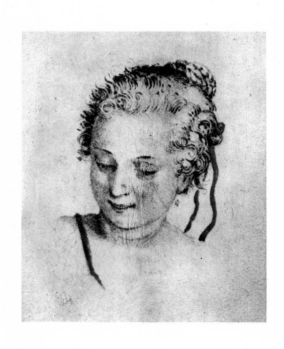

THE FEAST IN THE HOUSE OF LEVI

Academy, Venice
Photo Braun et Cⁱᵉ

THE FEAST IN THE HOUSE OF SIMON THE PHARISEE (Detail of Pl. 76)
Musée du Louvre, Paris
Photo Arch. Phot. d'Art et d'Hist.

THE FEAST IN THE HOUSE OF LEVI (Detail of Pl. 77)
Academy, Venice
Photo Braun et Cⁱᵉ

MARY MAGDALEN IN THE HOUSE OF SIMON THE PHARISEE

Regia Pinacoteca, Turin

Photo Brogi

THE FEAST IN THE HOUSE OF SIMON THE PHARISEE (Detail of Pl. 76)
Musée du Louvre, Paris
Photo Hyperion

HEAD OF A PILGRIM (Detail of Pl. 86)
Sanctuary, Monte Berico, Vicenza
Photo Alinari

PORTRAIT OF GRANO, A SERVITE FATHER (Detail of Pl. 86)
Sanctuary, Monte Berico, Vicenza
Photo Alinari

HEAD OF A CARDINAL (Detail of Pl. 86)
Sanctuary, Monte Berico, Vicenza
Photo Alinari

PORTRAIT OF ST. GREGORY (Detail of Pl. 86)
Sanctuary, Monte Berico, Vicenza
Photo Alinari

THE FEAST OF ST. GREGORY THE GREAT
Sanctuary, Monte Berico, Vicenza
Photo Alinari

CHRIST AT EMMAUS
Pinacothek, Dresden
Photo Braun et Cie

CHRIST AT EMMAUS
Musée du Louvre, Paris
Phot. Arch. Phot. d'Art et d'Hist.

CHRIST AT EMMAUS (Detail of Pl. 88)

Musée du Louvre, Paris
Photo Hyperion

THE PILGRIMS AT EMMAUS
Drawing. The Duke of Devonshire's Collection, Chatsworth
Photo Braun et Cie

90

THE WAY TO GOLGOTHA

Musée du Louvre, Paris

Photo Braun et Cie

ANGELS AND SAINTS

Drawing. Brera, Milan
Photo Braun et Cⁱᵉ

THE CRUCIFIXION
Pinacothek, Dresden
Photo Alinari

THE CRUCIFIXION
Drawing. Ambrosiana, Milan
Photo Braun et Cⁱᵉ

THE CRUCIFIXION
Pinacothek, Dresden
Photo Alinari

CALVARY
Drawing. Albertina, Vienna
Photo Braun et Cie

CALVARY
Musée du Louvre, Paris
Photo Hypérion

THE VIRGIN ENTHRONED
Drawing. Corsini, Florence
Photo Anderson

THE CORONATION OF THE VIRGIN
San Sebastiano, Venice
Photo Alinari

THE CORONATION OF THE VIRGIN
Academy, Venice
Photo Alinari

THE VIRGIN IN GLORY WITH SAINTS

San Sebastiano, Venice
Photo Alinari

THE MARTYRDOM OF A SAINT

Drawing. The Duke of Devonshire's Collection, Chatsworth
Photo Braun et Cie

THE MARTYRDOM OF ST. JUSTINA

S. Giustina, Padua
Photo Alinari

THE MARTYRDOM OF ST. MARK AND ST. MARCELLINUS

San Sebastiano, Venice
Photo Alinari

THE MARTYRDOM OF ST. JUSTINA
Uffizi, Florence
Photo Hyperion

THE MARTYRDOM OF ST. GENESIUS

Prado, Madrid
Photo Anderson

THE MARTYRDOM OF ST. GEORGE

San Giorgio in Braida, Verona

Photo Alinari

THE VISION OF ST. HELENA
Vatican Pinacoteca, Rome
Photo Alinari

THE VISION OF ST. HELENA

National Gallery, London
Photo Anderson

ST. JEROME IN THE DESERT

San Pietro Martire, Murano, Venice
Photo Alinari

THE MARTYRDOM OF ST. JULIAN

San Giuliano, Rimini
Photo Brogi

THE PENITENT MAGDALEN

Prado, Madrid

Photo Anderson

ST. CATHERINE
Uffizi, Florence
Photo Hyperion

ST. BENEDICT AND TWO OTHER SAINTS

Pitti, Florence
Photo Alinari

ST. PAUL
Uffizi, Florence
Photo Alinari

115

THE RAPE OF EUROPA
Doge's Palace, Anti-Collegio, Venice
Photo Alinari

THE RAPE OF EUROPA (Detail of Pl. 116)
Doge's Palace, Anti-Collegio, Venice
Photo Alinari

THE RAPE OF EUROPA (Detail of Pl. 116)
Doge's Palace, Anti-Collegio, Venice
Photo Alinari

118

THE RAPE OF EUROPA (Detail)
Capitol, Rome
Photo Alinari

119

VANITY

Accademia di S. Luca, Rome
Photo Alinari

JUPITER FULMINATING THE VICES

Musée du Louvre, Paris
Photo Hyperion

VENUS AND ADONIS

Prado, Madrid
Photo Anderson

MARS AND VENUS
The Italian Embassy, London
Photo Giraudon

CAIN WANDERING (Detail)
Prado, Madrid
Photo Anderson

JUPITER AND ANTIOPE
Pinacothek, Munich
Photo Braun 'et Cie

125

DANAE RECEIVING THE GOLDEN RAIN
Regia Pinacoteca, Turin
Photo Brogi

126

SUSANNA

Pinacothek, Dresden
Photo Alinari

BATHSHEBA

Lyons Museum
Photo Braun et Cie

SUSANNA AND THE ELDERS
Musée du Louvre, Paris
Photo Hypérion

THE CHASTE SUSANNA

Academia di S. Luca, Rome
Photo Alinari

SUSANNA AND THE ELDERS

Prado, Madrid

Photo Anderson

JUDITH
Caen Museum
Photo Braun et Cᴵᵉ

JUDITH

Palazzo Rosso, Genoa
Photo Alinari

SOLOMON AND THE QUEEN OF SHEBA

Regia Pinacoteca, Turin
Photo Brogi

SOLOMON AND THE QUEEN OF SHEBA (Detail of Pl. 134)
Regia Pinacoteca, Turin
Photo Brogi

ESTHER BEFORE AHASUERUS

Uffizi, Florence
Photo Alinari

ESTHER AND AHASUERUS
Musée du Louvre, Paris
Photo Hyperion

YOUTH AND AGE (Detail)

Doges Palace, Venice
Photo Alinari

HAPPY UNION

National Gallery, London
Photo Anderson

ALLEGORY OF PLENTY (Detail)
Academy, Venice
Photo Alinari

THE VIRGIN AND CHILD IN GLORY WITH SAINTS (Detail of Pl. 47)
Academy, Venice
Photo Alinari

THE SACRIFICE OF ISAAC
Prado, Madrid
Photo Anderson

THE FINDING OF MOSES

Prado, Madrid
Photo Anderson

THE FINDING OF MOSES
Dijon Museum
Photo Hanfstaengl

CHRIST AT EMMAUS (Detail of Pl. 88)

Musée du Louvre, Paris
Photo Hyperion

THE FAMILY OF DARIUS
Drawing. Weimar Museum
Photo Braun et Cⁱᵉ

THE FAMILY OF DARIUS BEFORE ALEXANDRE

National Gallery, London
Photo National Gallery

MAN AND CHILD
Drawing. Musée du Louvre, Paris
Photo Braun et C^{le}

FIVE ARMED MEN
Drawing. Uffizi, Florence
Photo Braun et C¹ᵉ

THE BATTLE OF LEPANTO

Academy, Venice
Photo Alinari

NYMPH AND SATYR

Drawing. Ecole des Beaux-Arts, Paris
Photo Giraudon

YOUTH BETWEEN VICE AND VIRTUE

Prado, Madrid
Photo Braun et Cⁱᵉ

CHRIST AT EMMAUS (Detail of Pl. 88)

Musée du Louvre, Paris
Photo Hyperion

THE TRIUMPH OF VENICE

Ceiling. Doge's Palace, Venice
Photo Alinari

THE TRIUMPH OF VENICE (Detail of Pl. 154)
Ceiling, Doge's Palace, Venice
Photo Anderson

MODERATION
Doge's Palace, Collegio, Venice
Photo Alinari

FORTUNE
Doge's Palace, Collegio, Venice
Photo Alinari

INDUSTRY

Doge's Palace, Collegio, Venice
Photo Alinari

PLENTY

Doge's Palace, Collegio, Venice
Photo Alinari

159

THE TRIUMPH OF VENICE (Detail of Pl. 154)
Ceiling. Doge's Palace, Venice
Photo Giraudon

PRINCIPAL MASTERPIECES OF VERONESE

AUSTRIA

VIENNA. — *Belvedere Museum* :

Adam and Eve and the first born. — The Annunciation. — The Adoration of the Magi. — St. Catherine and St. Barbara presenting two nuns to the Virgin and the Infant Christ. — The Mystic Marriage of St. Catherine. — Jesus and the Good Samaritan. — Christ and the Woman taken in adultery. — Christ before Jairus's House. — St. John the Baptist. — St. Sebastian. — St. Nicholas. — Judith carrying the head of Holophernus. — Venus and Cupid. — Venus and Adonis. — The Rape of Dejaneira. — Death of Lucretia. — Quintus Curtius throwing himself into the abyss. — Youth caressing a dog. — Portrait of Mark Anthony Barbaro. — Portrait of Catherine Cornaro. — Several other less important pictures.

BELGIUM

BRUSSELS. — *Royal Gallery* : Juno showering Gifts on Venice.

FRANCE

PARIS. — *Louvre* :

The Bath of Susanna. — The Flight from Sodom. — Esther before Ahasuerus. — Jupiter fulminating the Vices. — The Virgin with the Infant Christ and St. Catherine. — St. George. — The Virgin and the Infant Christ, surrounded by St. Joseph, St. Elizabeth, the Magdalen and a nun. — Jesus healing Peter's step-mother. — The Marriage at Cana. — Christ at Simon the Pharisee's. — Christ carrying the Cross. — Christ at Emmaus. — La Belle Nani. — Portrait of a Woman. — St. Mark crowning the Theological Virtues. — 18 drawings.

CAEN. — *The Museum* : The Temptation of St. Anthony. — The Israelites fleeing from Egypt.

DIJON. — *The Museum* : The Finding of Moses.

LILLE. — *The Museum* : The Martyrdom of St. George.

LYONS. — *The Museum* : The Bath of Bathsheba. — The Finding of Moses.

MONTPELLIER. — *The Museum* :

The Virgin amid Clouds. — The Mystic Marriage of St. Catherine. — St. Francis receiving the Stigmata.

RENNES. — *The Museum* : Perseus delivering Andromeda.

ROUEN. — *The Museum* : St. Barnabas healing the Sick.

GERMANY

BERLIN. — *Kaiser Friedrich Museum* :

Mars and Minerva. — Apollo and Juno. — Jupiter and Fortune. — Saturn on Olympus. — The Presentation in the Temple. — The Dead Christ. — The Finding of Moses. — Genii (4 canvases).

DARMSTADT. — The Marriage at Cana.

DRESDEN. — *State Picture Gallery*:

The Adoration of the Magi. — The Presentation in the Temple. — The Holy Family. — Jesus at Emmaus. — The Good Samaritan. — The Marriage at Cana. — The Virgin and the Cuccina Family. — Christ carrying the Cross. — Calvary. — The Resurrection. — Jesus and the Centurion. — The Finding of Moses. — Susanna and the Elders. — The Rape of Europa. — The Portrait of Daniel Barbaro (copy).

FRANKFORT. — *Museum*: Mars and Venus. — The Mystic Marriage of St. Catherine.

MUNICH. — *Old Pinacothek*:

Justice and Prudence. — Charity. — Faith. — Piety. — Force. — Temperance. — The rest on the Flight into Egypt. — Christ and the Adulteress. — Jesus and the Centurion. — Cupid holding chained dogs. — Portrait of a Woman. — The Death of Cleopatra.

GREAT BRITAIN

LONDON. — *National Gallery*:

The Vision of St. Helena. — The Consecration of St. Nicholas. — The Adoration of the Magi. — The Family of Darius before Alexander. — The Rape of Europa. — The Magdalen laying aside her Jewels.

EDINBURGH. — *National Gallery*: Mars and Venus. — Venus and Adonis.

DULWICH. — *Dulwich College*: A Saint blessing a Venetian Gentleman.

ITALY

FLORENCE. — *Uffizi Gallery*:

The Annunciation. — Esther. — The Holy Family. — The Virgin. — The Creation. — A Landscape. — The Martyrdom of St. Catherine. — A Self-Portrait.

Pitti Palace:

The Presentation of Christ in the Temple. — The three Marys at the Tomb. — Christ taking leave of His Mother. — The Portrait of Veronese's Wife. — Several Portraits.

GENOA. — *The Museum*: The Martyrdom of St. Justina.

MANTUA. — *The Cathedral*: The Temptation of St. Anthony.

MILAN. — *The Brera Museum*:

Christ in the House of Simon the Pharisee (replica of the picture in the Louvre). — St. Cornelius, Pope. — Adoration of the Magi. — The Baptism of Christ. — Christ in the Garden of Olives. — St. Anthony enthroned between St. Cornelius and St. Cyprian. — The Marriage at Cana (small replica).

NAPLES. — *Museum*: The Coronation of a Venetian Doge.

PADUA. — *The Church of St. Justina*: The Martyrdom of St. Justina.

ROME. — *The Borghese Gallery*: The Parable of the Fish.

The Capitoline Museum: The Rape of Europa.

The Quirinal: St. Sebastian.

The Vatican Museum: St. Helena.

TREVISO. — *Masiera Palace*:

The Planets. — The Earth. — The Four Elements. — The Four Seasons. — Maternal Love. — Glory crowning Merit. — Time and History. — Cupid conquering Force. — Virtue repelling Vice. — Married Love.

TURIN. — *The Museum*:

The Finding of Moses. — Christ in the House of Simon the Pharisee (another version of the picture in the Louvre). — The Queen of Sheba before Solomon.

VENICE. — *The Accademia* :

The Virgin enthroned with the Infant Christ. — The Annunciation. — The Flagellation of St. Christina. — The Victory of the Venetians over the Turks. — The Coronation of the Virgin. — The Assumption. — St. Mark and St. Matthew. — The Feast of Levi the Publican. — The Supper of Simon the Leper. — The Mystic Marriage of St. Catherine.

The Doge's Palace :

Hall of the Grand Council : The Apotheosis of Venice. — The Defense of Scutari. — The Taking of Smyrna. — The Return of the Doge Contarini, after the Victory of Chioggia. — Departure of Pope Alexander III's envoys for Pavia. — Time revealing Truth.

Hall of the Anticollegio : The Rape of Europa.

Hall of the College : The Victory of Lepanto. — St. Mark, Faith, Justice, Peace (ceiling). — The Saviour in His Glory. — Moderation. — Industry. — Vigilance. — Prudence. — Fortune. — Fidelity. — Simplicity. — Several allegories. — Neptune and Mars.

Hall of the Chiefs : An Angel chasing the Vices.

The Librarian's Room : The Adoration of the Magi.

Other Halls :

Venice surrounded by Hercules, Ceres and Genii. — Christ in the Garden of Olives. — Institution of the Rosary by St. Dominic. — Age and Youth. — Venus contemplating Olympus. — Juno scattering Gifts on Venice. — Music. — Geometry. — Arithmetic. — The Apotheosis of Honour.

The Convent of the Servites : Christ in the House of Simon.

Church of St. Andrew : St. Jerome in the Desert.

Church of the Holy Apostles : The Miracle of the Manna.

Church of St. Barnabas : The Holy Family.

Church of St. Catherine : The Mystic Marriage of St. Catherine.

Church of San Fermo Maggiore : The Madonna with St. John the Baptist and St. Zeno.

Church of San Francesco della Vigna : The Resurrection. — The Madonna with Angels. — The Virgin with Saints.

Church of San Giovanni in Latizana : The Baptism of Christ.

Church of San Giacoma : St. Laurence, St. Mark and St. Augustine. — The Four Theological Virtues. — The Four Doctors of the Church.

Church of St. John and St. Paul : The Nativity.

Church of St. Julian : The Dead Christ supported by Angels. — The Last Supper.

Church of St. Luke : St. Luke writing his Gospel.

Library of St. Mark : A Ceiling.

Church of St. Paul : The Marriage of the Virgin.

Church of St. Sebastian : The Coronation of the Virgin. — The Story of Esther (four panels). — Prophets. — Sibyls. — Scenes from the life and death of St. Sebastian. — Purification of the Virgin. — The Probationary Bath. — The Crucifixion.

VERONA. — *Church of San Giorgio in Braida* : The Martyrdom of St. George. — The Madonna of the Marogna Family.

VICENZA. — *Chierati Palace* : The Feast of St. Gregory.

Convent of Monte Berico : The Feast of St. Gregory.

RUSSIA

LENINGRAD. — *The Hermitage :*

The Holy Family. — The Flight into Egypt. — The Adoration of the Magi. — Lazarus and the rich man. — Christ among the Doctors. — The Dead Christ supported by the Virgin and an Angel. — The Mystic Marriage of St. Catherine. — Diana and Minerva. — Mars and Venus. — The Finding of Moses. — Portrait of a Man. — Various sketches.

The Leuchtenberg Gallery : The Widow of the Spanish Ambassador in Venice presenting her son to Philip II.

SPAIN

MADRID. — *Prado Museum :*

Venus and Adonis. — Susanna and the Elders. — Portrait of a young Woman holding gloves. — Portrait of a young Woman with a dog. — Portrait of a young Woman wearing a golden girdle. — Portrait of a young Woman. — Portrait of an old Lady. — The Adoration of the Magi. — The Infant Christ and the Virgin. — Jesus among the Doctors. — Jesus and the Centurion (variant). — Christ at the Marriage of Cana. — The Woman taken in Adultery. — The Calvary. — The Martyrdom of St. Genesius. — The Penitent Magdalen. — Youth between Vice and Virtue. — The Sacrifice of Abraham. — Cain wandering with his Family. — The Finding of Moses.

SWEDEN

STOCKHOLM. — *National Museum :* The Circumcision. — The Magdalen. — The Holy Family. — A Madonna.

BIBLIOGRAPHY

I. SOURCES

BOSCHINI : *Il ricche minere.* Venice 1674.

RIDOLFI : *Le Meraviglie dell' arte.* Venice 1674.

G. VASARI : *Vie des Peintres.* Translated into French by Lechanclé, Paris, 1840

ZUCCARO : *Idea de' pittori, scultori et architetti.* Turin 1607.

II. STANDARD WORKS.

ADELN : *Caliari.* Article in " Allgemeines Lexikon ".

B.BERENSON : *The Italian Painters of the Renaissance.* Oxford University Press, new ed. 1932.

G. LAFENESTRE : *La Peinture Italienne.* Paris, 1885.

André MICHEL : *Histoire de l'Art.* Paris, 1905. Article by André Peraté, vol. V, Part 2, page 532.

MOLMENTI : *Vie privée de Venise.* Venise, 1895.

E. MUNTZ : *Histoire de l'Art pendant la Renaissance.* Paris, 1889-1891.

LUIGI PELAUDI : *Cento Capolavori della rinascenza italiana.* Bergamo, 1911.

G. ROUCHES : *La peinture au Musée du Louvre. Ecoles italiennes,* XVIe, XVIIe, XVIIIe siècles. Paris, undated.

Corrado RICCI : *Italie du Nord.* Paris, 1885.

ZANNANDREIS : *Le vite dei pittori... veronesi :* Verona, 1891.

III. SPECIAL WORKS.

A. BASCHET : *Paul Véronèse devant le Saint Office.* Gazette des Beaux-Arts, vol. 3, III, p. 378.

A. BELL : *Paolo Veronese.* London, 1905.

G. BIADEGO : *Intorno a Paolo Veronese.* Venice, 1899.

Charles BLANC : *Histoires de Peintres.* Paris.

Charles BLANC : *Les fresques du Véronèse au château de Masère près de Trévise.*

P. CALIARO : *Paolo Veronese.* Rome, 1888.

R. FRY : *Paolo Veronese.* Bielefeld, 1896.

P. LEFORT : *Les fresques du Véronèse au Musée de Madrid.* Gazette des Beaux-Arts, 1, vol. XXIII, p. 378.

MEISSNER : *Paolo Veronese.* Bielefeld, 1897.

Ch. YRIARTE : *Paul Véronèse.* Paris, 1888.

LIST OF PLATES

33. Portrait of a Young Woman. Canvas, 1,15 m. by 0,95 m. Musée du Louvre, Paris. Photo Hypérion.

34. Self-Portrait, Canvas, 0,47 m. by 0,39 m. Uffizi, Florence.

35. Portrait of Daniele Barbaro. Canvas, 1,37 m. by 2 m. Pitti, Florence. Photo Alinari.

36. Portrait of Daniele Barbaro. Canvas, 1.32 m. by 1.02 m. Pinacothek, Dresden. Photo Alinari.

37. Portrait of Pacio Guarienti. Canvas. Museo Civico, Verona. Photo Alinari.

38. Madonna with the Cuccina Family. Canvas, 1.47 m. by 4.16 m. Pinacothek, Dresden. Photo Braun & C^{le}.
Head of a Negro. Drawing. Musée du Louvre. Photo Giraudon.

39. The Adoration of the Magi. Canvas, 2.04 m. by 4.55 m. Pinacothek, Dresden. Photo Braun & C^{le}.
Cat and Dogs. Red chalk and India-ink. Academy, Venice. Photo Braun & C^{le}.

40. Madonna with the Cuccina Family. Detail of plate 38. Photo Braun & C^{le}.

41. The Marriage at Cana. Detail of Plate 71. Musée du Louvre, Paris. Photo Hyperion.

42. The Annunciation. Canvas. Chapter Rooms, Escorial, Madrid. Photo Anderson.

43. The Annunciation. Canvas, 3.94 m. by 1.94 m. Academy, Venice. Photo Alinari.

44. The Archangel of the Annunciation. Detail. The painting (canvas) measures 2.70 m. by 1.04 m. Academy, Venice. Photo Alinari.

45. The Virgin of the Annunciation. Detail. (See plate 44, above). Photo Alinari.

46. The Adoration of the Magi. Canvas, half-linen, 4.20 m. by 4.20 m. Academy, Venice. Photo Alinari.

47. The Virgin and Child in Glory with Saints. Canvas, 3.90 m. by 2.15 m. Academy, Venice. Photo Alinari.

48. The Holy Family. Canvas on wood, 0.51 m. by 0.43 m. Musée du Louvre, Paris. Photo Arch. Phot. d'Art et d'Hist.

49. The Holy Family. Canvas, 0.90 m. by 0.90 m. Musée du Louvre, Paris. Photo Hyperion.

50. The Virgin and Child with St. Anthony. Canvas. San Sebastiano, Venice. Photo Alinari.
Study of a Head.

51. The Holy Family with St. Barbara. Canvas, 0.97 m. by 1.79 m. Uffizi, Florence. Photo Alinari.
The Virgin and Child with St. Catherine. Drawing. Uffizi, Florence. Photo Alinari.

52. The Holy Family with Angels making Music. Drawing. Musée du Louvre, Paris. Photo Giraudon.

53. The Rest on the Flight into Egypt. Drawing. British Museum. Photo Braun & C^{le}.

54. The Marriage of St. Catherine. Two Angels. Detail of Plate 56.

55. The Marriage of St. Catherine. St. Catherine. Detail of Plate 56.

56. The Marriage of St. Catherine. Canvas. S. Catarina, Venice. Photo Alinari.

57. The Marriage of St. Catherine. Canvas, 1.28 m. by 1.29 m. Museum of Montpellier. Photo Hyperion.

58. The Marriage of St. Catherine. Canvas, 0.65 m. by 0.90 m. Antoine Orliac collection, Paris. Photo P. Delbo.

59. Jesus among the Doctors. Canvas, 2.36 m. by 4.30 m. Prado, Madrid. Photo Anderson.

60. Christ and the Centurion. Canvas, 1.78 m. by 2.75 m. Pinacothek, Dresden. Photo Braun & Cie.

61. Christ and the Centurion. Canvas, 1.43 m. by 1.36 m. Prado, Madrid. Photo Anderson.

62. Historical Scene. Drawing. British Museum. Photo Braun & C^{le}.
Studies of Heads.

63. Head of a Man. Drawing. British Museum. Photo Braun & C^{le}.

64. St. John in the Wilderness. Canvas, 2.08 m. by 1.40 m. Villa Borghese, Rome. Photo Alinari.

65. The Baptism of Christ. Canvas, 1.93 m. by 1.32 m. Pitti, Florence. Photo Hyperion.

66. The Marriage at Cana. Drawing. Weimar Museum. Photo Braun & C^{le}.
Study of a Head.

67. The Marriage at Cana. Canvas, 2.05 m. by 4.55 m. Pinacothek, Dresden. Photo Braun & C^{le}.
Study of a Head. Drawing. The Duke of Devonshire's collection, Chatsworth. Photo Braun & C^{le}.

68. The Marriage at Cana. Head of a Guest. Detail of Plate 67. Photo Alinari.

69. The Marriage at Cana. Head of Christ. Detail of Plate 67. Photo Alinari.

70. The Marriage at Cana. Canvas, 1.27 m. by 2.09 m. Prado, Madrid. Photo Anderson.

71. The Marriage at Cana. Canvas, 6.66 m. by 9.90 m. Musée du Louvre, Paris. Photo Braun & C^{le}.

72. The Marriage at Cana. Group of Musicians. Detail of Plate 71. Photo Braun & Cie.

73. The Marriage at Cana. Detail of Plate 71. Photo Hyperion.

74. The Marriage at Cana. Detail of Plate 71. Photo Alinari.

75. The Marriage at Cana. Detail of Plate 71. Photo Alinari.

76. The Feast in the House of Simon the Pharisee. Canvas, 4.54 m. by 9.74 m. Musée du Louvre, Paris. Photo Arch. Phot. d'Art et d'Hist. Study of a Head.

77. The Feast in the House of Levi. Canvas, 5.50 m. by 12.78 m. Academy, Venice. Photo Braun & Cie. Study of a Head.

78. The Feast in the House of Simon the Pharisee. Detail of Plate 76. Photo Arch. Phot. d'Art et d'Hist.

79. The Feast in the House of Levi. The Nobleman in Green Silk. Detail of Plate 77. Photo Braun & Cie.

80. Mary Magdalen in the House of Simon the Pharisee. Canvas, 3.15 m. by 4.51 m. Regia Pinacoteca, Turin. Photo Brogi.

81. The Feast in the House of Simon the Pharisee. Detail of Plate 76. Musée du Louvre, Paris. Photo Hyperion.

82. The Feast of St. Gregory the Great. Head of a Pilgrim. Detail of Plate 86. Sanctuary, Monte Berico, Vicenza. Photo Alinari.

83. The Feast of St. Gregory the Great. Portrait of Grano, a Servite Father. Detail of Plate 86. Photo Alinari.

84. The Feast of St. Gregory the Great. Head of a Cardinal. Detail of plate 86. Photo Alinari.

85. The Feast of St. Gregory the Great. Portrait of St. Gregory. Detail of Plate 86. Photo Alinari.

86. The Feast of St. Gregory the Great. Canvas. Sanctuary, Monte Berico, Vicenza. Photo Alinari.

87. Christ at Emmaus. Canvas, 1.20 m. by 1.81 m. Pinacothek, Dresden. Photo Braun & Cie.

88. Christ at Emmaus. Canvas, 2.90 m. by 4.48 m. Musée du Louvre, Paris. Photo Arch. Phot. d'Art et d'Hist.

89. Christ at Emmaus. Children. Detail of Plate 88. Photo Hyperion.

90. The Pilgrims at Emmaus. Drawing. The Duke of Devonshire's collection, Chatsworth. Photo Braun & Cie.

91. The Way to Golgotha. Wood, 0.58 m. by 0.35 m. Musée du Louvre. Paris. Photo Braun & Cie.

92. Angels and Saints. Drawing. Brera, Milan. Photo Braun & Cie.

93. The Crucifixion. Canvas, 0.98 m. by 0.76 m. Pinacothek, Dresden. Photo Alinari.

94. The Crucifixion. Drawing. Ambrosiana, Milan. Photo Braun & Cie.

95. The Crucifixion. Canvas, Pinacothek, Dresden. Photo Alinari.

96. Calvary. The Holy Women. Drawing. Albertina, Vienna. Photo Braun & Cie.

97. Calvary. Canvas, 1.02 m. by 1.02 m. Musée du Louvre. Paris. Photo Hyperion.

98. The Virgin enthroned. Drawing. Corsini, Florence. Photo Anderson.

99. The Coronation of the Virgin. Canvas. San Sebastiano, Venice. Photo Alinari.

100. The Coronation of the Virgin. Canvas, 3.90 m. by 2.15 m. Academy, Venice. Photo Alinari.

101. The Virgin in Glory with Saints. Canvas. San Sebastiano, Venice. Photo Alinari.

102. The Martyrdom of a Saint. Drawing. The Duke of Devonshire's collection, Chatsworth. Photo Braun & Cie.

103. The Martyrdom of St. Justina. Canvas. S. Giustina, Padua. Photo Alinari.

104. The Martyrdom of St. Mark and St. Marcellinus. Canvas. San Sebastiano, Venice. Photo Alinari.

105. The Martyrdom of St. Justina. Canvas, 0.89 m. by 1.02 m. Uffizi, Florence. Photo Hyperion.

106. The Martyrdom of St. Genesius. Canvas, 2.48 m. by 1.82 m. Prado, Madrid. Photo Anderson.

107. The Martyrdom of St. George. Canvas. San Giorgio in Braida, Verona. Photo Alinari.

108. The Vision of St. Helena. Canvas, 0.465 m. by 0.345 m. Vatican Pinacoteca, Rome. Photo Alinari.

109. The Vision of St. Helena. Canvas, 1.96 m. by 1.14 m. National Gallery, London. Photo Anderson.

110. St. Jerome in the Desert. Canvas. San Pietro Martire, Murano, Venice. Photo Alinari.

111. The Martyrdom of St. Julian. Canvas. San Giuliano, Rimini. Photo Brogi.

112. The Penitent Magdalen. Canvas, 1.22 m. by 1.05 m. Prado, Madrid. Photo Anderson.

113. St. Catherine. Canvas, 0.77 m. by 0.62 m. Uffizi, Florence. Photo Hyperion.

114. St. Benedict and two other Saints. Canvas. Pitti, Florence. Photo Alinari.

115. St. Paul. Canvas. Uffizi, Florence. Photo Alinari.

116. The Rape of Europa. Canvas, 2.50 m. by 3 m. Doge's Palace, Anti-Collegio, Venice. Photo Alinari.

117. The Rape of Europa. Detail of Plate 116. Photo Alinari.

118. The Rape of Europa. Detail of Plate 116. Photo Alinari.

119. The Rape of Europa. Detail. The painting (canvas) measures 3.10 m. by 2.44 m. Capitol, Rome. Photo Alinari.

120. Vanity. Canvas, life-size. Accademia di S. Luca, Rome. Photo Alinari.

121. Jupiter fulminating the Vices. Oval canvas, 5,60 m. by 3,30 m. Musée du Louvre, Paris. Photo Hyperion.

122. Venus and Adonis. Canvas, 2.12 m. by 1.91 m. Prado, Madrid. Photo Anderson.

123. Mars and Venus. Canvas, 0.47 m. by 0.475 m. The Italian Embassy, London. Photo Giraudon.

166

124. Cain wandering. Detail. The painting (canvas) measures 1.05 m. by 1.53 m. Prado, Madrid. Photo Anderson.

125. Jupiter and Antiope. Canvas on wood, 0.60 m. by 0.49 m. Pinacothek, Munich. Photo Braun & Cie.

126. Danae receiving the Golden Rain. Canvas. Royal Gallery, Turin. Photo Brogi.
Study of a Head.

127. Susanna. Canvas, 1.25 m. by 1.04 m. Pinacothek, Dresden. Photo Alinari.

128. Bathsheba. Canvas, 2.27 m. by 2.37 m. Lyons Museum. Photo Braun & Cie.

129. Susanna and the Elders. Canvas, 1.98 m. by 1.98 m. Musée du Louvre, Paris. Photo Hyperion.

130. The Chaste Susanna. Canvas. Accademia di S. Luca, Rome. Photo Alinari.

131. Susanna and the Elders. Canvas, 1.51 m. by 1.77 m. Prado, Madrid. Photo Anderson.

132. Judith. Canvas, 2.45 m. by 2.69 m. Caen Museum. Photo Braun & Cie.
Study of a Head.

133. Judith. Canvas. Palazzo Rosso, Genoa. Photo Alinari.

134. Solomon and the Queen of Sheba. Canvas, 3.44 m. by 5.45 m. Regia Pinacoteca, Turin. Photo Brogi.

135. Solomon and the Queen of Sheba. Detail of Plate 134. Photo Brogi.

136. Esther before Ahasuerus. Canvas, 1.14 m. by 1.78 m. Uffizi, Florence. Photo Alinari.

137. Esther and Ahasuerus. Canvas, 2 m. by 3.10 m. Musée du Louvre, Paris. Photo Hyperion.

138. Youth and Age. Detail: Youth. Fragment of ceiling panel. Doge's Palace, Venice. Photo Alinari.

139. Happy Union. Allegorical group. Canvas, 1.86 m. by 1.86 m. National Gallery, London. Photo Anderson.

140. Allegory of Plenty. Detail. Academy, Venice. Photo Alinari.

141. The Virgin and Child in Glory with Saints. Detail of Plate 47. Academy, Venice. Photo Alinari.

142. The Sacrifice of Isaac. Canvas, 1.29 m. by 0.95 m. Prado, Madrid. Photo Anderson.

143. The Finding of Moses. Canvas, 0.56 m. by 0.43 m. Prado, Madrid. Photo Anderson.

144. The Finding of Moses. Canvas, 1.22 m. by 1.68 m. Dijon Museum. Photo Hanfstaengl.

145. Christ at Emmaus. Detail of Plate 88. Musée du Louvre, Paris. Photo Hyperion.

146. The Family of Darius before Alexander. Drawing. Weimar Museum. Photo Braun & Cie.
Study of a Head.

147. The Family of Darius before Alexander. Canvas, 2.34 m. by 4.73 m. National Gallery, London. Photo National Gallery.
Study of a Head.

148. Man and Child. Drawing. Musée du Louvre, Paris. Photo Braun & Cie.

149. Five Armed Men. Drawing. Uffizi, Florence. Photo Braun & Cie.

150. The Battle of Lepanto. Canvas, 1.67 m. by 1.37 m. Academy, Venice. Photo Alinari.

151. Nymph and Satyr. Drawing. École des Beaux-Arts, Paris. Photo Giraudon.

152. Youth between Vice and Virtue. Canvas, 1.01 m. by 1.74 m. Prado, Madrid. Photo Braun & Cie.

153. Christ at Emmaus. Detail of Plate 88. Musée du Louvre, Paris. Photo Hyperion.

154. The Triumph of Venice. Ceiling. Doge's Palace, Venice. Photo Alinari.

155. The Triumph of Venice. Detail of ceiling. Photo Anderson.

156. Moderation. Canvas. Doge's Palace, Collegio, Venice. Photo Alinari.

157. Fortune. Canvas. Doge's Palace, Collegio, Venice. Photo Alinari.

158. Industry. Canvas. Doge's Palace, Collegio, Venice. Photo Alinari.

159. Plenty. Canvas. Doge's Palace, Collegio, Venice. Photo Alinari.

160. The Triumph of Venice. Detail of ceiling. Doge's Palace, Venice. Photo Alinari.

CONTENTS